Facing the *IF* in Life

Bob Shephard

Facing the *IF* in Life

Bob Shephard

Copyright © 2015 Bob Shephard

ISBN: 978-0692393123

Printed in the United States of America.

Published by Rebel Key, Tulsa OK

Thank you --- To my wife, Faith, for her encouragement to author another book. Also to all the readers of my 1st book, *Unprepared*, who have been asking for another. To Tami for typing the manuscript, to Ed and Mackenzi for the cover design, and to all my family & friends for their support.

Table of Contents

Preface

Facing the *IF* in Life is dedicated to anyone who has experienced the mental gymnastics that *if* can cause. Be they positive or negative mind exercises, *if* can be a relentless catalyst for energy consumption in any of us. My intentions in writing would be to help us choose positive responses to the possibilities with the help of Biblical truths and real life experiences. If Facing the *IF* in Life can cause us to realize we have a choice in how we respond or even react when we hear *if*, then the book will accomplish its purpose. Hopefully, it will also encourage the reader to know he or she does not have to face the *if* in life alone! There is One available to help. There is wisdom, and truth, even promises clearly communicated in the Bible that will help us in our decisions, if we choose to consider them. You can receive the help you need to face life's *ifs*. You can gain the courage to make positive choices. You can have peace when *if* confronts you. It is your choice. May the *ifs* in life lead you to conscious, positive possibilities. May you know you can face the *ifs* in life without torment or loss of sleep. The following chapters will address some of the *ifs* in life and give you insights to help you make your choices regarding *if*.

- 1 -

The Complexity of *IF*

Do you ever have moments where you wished *if* wasn't part of your vocabulary? Maybe when you have been devalued or driven to the dark side of your mind where fear and negativity rule over every decision you choose to make.

If may be the biggest two letter word one can have in his or her vocabulary. *If* will play heart and mind games with you your whole life; oh, the complexity of the *if* in life! When you couple *what* or *only* with *if* (what if or if only) we can see positive possibilities and choose to act, or we can withdraw into a paralysis state because of the fears of *what if* or the regrets of *if only*. Put *as* with *if* (as if) and we usually get mind videos that may produce seemingly real images that are on continuous play. Remember, that *if* is virtual.

So how did *if* get to be such an ingrained part of our thinking? How did two letters *i* and *f* when joined together become the power word *if*? A simplistic answer would be they were placed in the middle of life! So right in the middle of life, we have to be face to face with *if*. The mystery of the power or the effect of *if* on your life can only be assessed by you, by your closest friends, or by God. Regardless of how you reach this realization, you will have to face the *if* in life. Resolving *if* based on God's words will bring you peace, healing and hope.

Facing the *if* in life starts at a very young age in every one of us. We may not remember how early in our own lives, but we can observe a baby and see *if* being confronted and choices being made. For example, observe a baby learning to feed himself or herself with a spoon. The baby may be placed in a high chair (1st clue *if* is coming), receive a spoon (*if* is getting closer), have a bib tied around his or her neck (*if* is almost here), and then the baby dish of food is placed in front of him or her (it is decision time about *if*). The baby's stomach, eyes, and senses say it is time to choose. The thought process may be something like this: If I am going to eat with the spoon, I need to choose to pick it up. If I want food, I must put it in the dish of food, lift up the spoon with food to my mouth, insert it into my mouth and if I like it, do it again! Or watch an infant facing *if* and the choices involved when it comes to learning to walk. "If I could pull myself upright, if I could stand, if I could pick my foot up and place it forward, (and still stand) then the other foot, etc. But if I fall it will hurt, maybe even more than just the landing jolt. If I hurt my arm or hand, I might not be able to feed myself. The risk of falling seems very high since I've never walked before and I don't want to starve to death because I couldn't feed myself. Hmm, hmm. Maybe I should pass on this learning to walk...." *if*? (Silly, isn't it?) But my point is at a very early age *if* becomes so much a part of us that at times our behavior no longer considers other ramifications of that little two letter word that is such a complex part of our life and our life choices. Sometimes out of behavioral repetition we do not consciously consider our own choices concerning *if*. This may be interpreted as being over-confident or maybe even prideful arrogance in some cases. It is critically vital to consider consciously our choices concerning *if*. The unconscious behavioral choices regarding *if* are just the opposite of the ones that cause us to be paranoid about the *if* in life every time it presents itself. Too often fear dominates this person's response presenting a myriad of negative possibilities resulting in a choice that paralyzes the person to do nothing because the risks are too great.

The apostle Paul and his companions had traveled to Pisidian Antioch where on the Sabbath they went to the synagogue to worship. The rulers of the synagogue sent word to Paul and his traveling companions saying,

> Brothers, if you have a message of encouragement for the people, please speak
>
> — Acts 13:15

So like Paul, I bring to your thinking that God gave you and me choice. We choose how we face the *if* in life. The encouraging words are that we do not have to do that alone. The Holy Spirit is with us, available to guide and comfort us, to give us courage to choose the positive even if there is some pain or heartache involved. Remember, if God sends you pain with your *if* in life, it is so you will understand His purpose! The following chapter will present a variety of *ifs* that people I have pastored faced in life or that my wife and I have faced. As you read further my prayer would be that consciously you will choose to face the *if* in your life as it presents itself. Make the choice guided by God's Holy Spirit. May you have the courage to do so and receive real peace, no more pothering. When you make your choice with God's help the most powerful two letter word, *if*, will no longer be able to hold you captive or keep you powerless. You will be able to face the *if* in life. Your mind and heart will know peace and positive possibilities produce good fruit in your life.

- 2 -

Pruned *If* You Do, Pruned *If* You Don't

Think on pruned *if* you do, pruned *if* you don't and the power of the catalytic *if* will keep you awake for a while. Allow me to be your gardener guide in this chapter so that you will consider to choose and produce good fruit in your life.

Have you ever purchased produce that looked good on the outside of the bag, the part you could see, but when you got it home and opened the bag you found spoiled, inedible, rotten fruit? Good fruit comes from trees or vines that have been pruned. They have been attended to so that fruit can form and mature to the place it is ready for harvest. If it has been cared for properly, it will be good for its intended use. The whole process involves many steps but one key step is the pruning of the tree or the vine. If you have ever grown your own tomatoes you know how important it is to prune off the "sucker" branches from the main trunk. The same is true with fruit trees; they need pruning to produce large, healthy fruit.

The Bible has a lot to say about pruning and producing good fruit. Jesus says,

> I am the true vine, and my Father is the gardener. He cuts
> off every branch in me that bears no fruit, while every
> branch that does bear fruit he prunes *(the Greek word also
> means cleans)* so that it will be even more fruitful.
>
> — John 15:1-2

So you will be "pruned if you do and pruned if you don't," cleaned for His service. The Gardener wants us to bear good fruit for the kingdom of God. The Gardener inspects the tree or the vine and prunes based on what He sees. He looks for the Fruit of the Spirit:

> love, joy, peace, patience, goodness, faithfulness,
> gentleness, and self-control.
>
> — Galatians 5:22

If He finds this kind of fruit, His actions of pruning are more cleansing and trimming away of any developing "sucker" branches or shoots that would try to take us back to the sinful, selfish nature. That nature produces obvious sinful fruit:

> sexual immorality, impurity, debauchery, idolatry,
> witchcraft, hatred, discord, jealousy, fits of rage, selfish
> ambition, dissensions, factions, envy, drunkenness,
> orgies..."
>
> — Galatians 5:14-21

Selfish indulgences based on the sinful nature's desires are all fruits of a person living to gratify self. You see, the wild "sucker" shoots will produce bad fruit, whereas the pruned tree or vine has been grafted into God's Spirit to produce the good fruit. The Gardner doesn't give the tree or vine a choice to the type of pruning he will do once He has inspected the fruit, the tree, or the vine. God, the Father, the master Gardner, gives us opportunities to look at our fruit and decide whether or not we will allow radical pruning so that His Spirit is in control—not our spirit. He gives us choice. You and I decide what kind of fruit will be produced, then the Gardener starts His pruning.

Jesus tells this parable:

> A man had a fig tree, planted in his vineyard, and he went to look for fruit on it, but did not find any. So he said to the man who took care of the vineyard, "for three years now I've been coming to look for fruit on this fig tree and haven't found any. Cut it down. Why should it use up the soil?"
>
> "Sir," the man replied, "leave it alone for one more year, and I'll dig around it and fertilize it. If it bears fruit next year, fine! If not, then cut it down."
> — Luke 13:6-9

Maybe someone is reading this and thinking what good fruit has ever come from my life? If God has been checking us out for good fruit but hasn't found any, maybe this book is being used by the Holy Spirit to say, "give him or her a little more time," God. Time to surrender and bear good fruit, the fruit of His Spirit, fruit that will last.

If you are a "church-goer," but are void of good fruit, ask yourself who is in control of your life? Maybe you have been hurt in the vineyard by other careless church-goers or even a pastor. You may just need to take time and heal. Let Dr. Jesus make a heart call. The last thing the world needs today is one more sick "church-goer" operating as a wounded healer producing blemished fruit that spoils quickly, and contaminates anyone or anything it touches.

Choose to be pruned to produce good fruit.

Blessed is the man who does not walk in the counsel of the wicked or stand in the way of sinners or sit in the seat of mockers. But his delight is in the law of the Lord, and on his law he meditates day and night. He is like a tree planted by streams of water which yields its fruit in season and whose leaf does not wither. Whatever he does prospers.

— Psalms 1:1-3

The fruit of the righteous is a tree of life, and he who wins souls is wise.

— Proverbs 13:30

The Bible clearly states:

By their fruit you will recognize them. *(The surrendered, Spirit-filled followers of Jesus).* Do people pick grapes from thorn bushes, or figs from thistles? Likewise every good tree bears good fruit, but a bad tree bears bad fruit. A good tree cannot bear bad fruit, and a bad tree cannot bear good fruit. Every tree that does not bear good fruit is cut down and thrown into the fire. Thus by their fruit you will recognize them.

— Matthew 7:16-20

The Bible makes it very clear that we need to decide to have the Master Gardner prune us so that we by His Spirit can produce good fruit for the Kingdom of God. Fruit that is without blemish so that others may choose to know the Master Gardner, be filled by His Spirit, and not be lost for eternity. Fruit that is not contaminated on the inside. Even though the outside may look really good, we know what a bad taste we get when we bite into good looking fruit only to find the inside rotten. Pruning is necessary. The more we allow God to prune us, the more we see the fruit of the Spirit at work in us. Let Him prune you, heal you and love you. He will! When you do, the pruning will begin. You will produce good fruit from the inside out. As you make prayerful choices, God will make the changes so that you are able to love unconditionally, to have peace, to be patient, to be kind, gentle, joyful, faithful, good, and even have self-control. Good fruit is in your future if you choose to let Him prune you, if you face up to the control issue and let Him be in control of you. The result is good fruit from you and for you.

The fact is *if* you are reading this, God is still giving you time to choose. You can be a new person, producing good fruit. You can be "grafted in" to the tree that produces good fruit. Fruit that lasts for an eternity. Our time here is so temporary; James compares it to a "vapor" or "mist." (James 4:14-15) We are here for a relatively, very short time, especially compared to eternity. While we are here, we are to produce good fruit. Fruit that will last, even after we are gone.

As you inspect your fruit (what your life is producing), is it good? Would your friends or family say you are a positive, contributing influence for good? You can be! Allow the Gardner to prune you because you ask. Don't wait until you have no choice regarding the pruning and eternity.

May the fruit of your life be good. May the fruit of your life have a healthy, positive impact on those closest to you. May the good fruit of your life spill over onto others you may encounter in life! May your choices be good choices. Your choices produce seeds. Seeds produce a crop. Therefore good choices produce good seeds that produce a good crop. The Bible clearly states "a man reaps what he sows." (Galatians 6:9) *If* he or she sows bad choices, the result is bad. But we can choose to make good choices and receive good results.

- 3 -

Does *If* Keep You Awake?

Is there an *if* in your mind that is terrorizing you? Does it keep you awake at night? How long has it been since you had a good night's sleep? Does the *if* keep you so fatigued or zoned out that your daily tasks suffer? Has *if* joined *what* so that you are monopolized by *what if* 24/7? Allow me to touch on a few of the *what ifs* that are common terrorists for us. If does not have to be such a pother that we tremble each time *what if* flashes through our mind. You can choose to answer your *what if* with faith and trust.

Maybe you can identify with some of these terrorizing *what ifs*. Have you heard any one of these terrorists?

- What if being connected is a real disconnect?

- What if you need emotional or spiritual healing?

- What if a relative has recently become too relative?

- What if "overwhelmed" is the best word to describe you?

- What if you realize instant gratification is what motivates your choices?

- What if you have faced unholy holiness?

- What if you have been devalued?

- What if your career owns you?

- What if the word responsibility causes alarm or makes you feel guilty?

- What if you have lost purpose or maybe never really found it?

- What if it smells like smoke regarding your choices?

- What if toxic describes your thoughts?

- What if the pursuit of pleasure is no longer pleasurable?

- What if life's trials overshadow life's successes?

- What if decisions (past, present, or future) keep you immobilized?

- What if everything you hear seems like "bad news"?

- What if you feel forgotten and alone?

- What if the fear of failure is always your first thought?

- What if the stock market crashes, the economy goes south, and your assets are worthless?

- What if you lose your job?

- What if your best friend or wife leaves?

- What if the Bible is true?

- What if Jesus is the son of God, the Messiah, yes, the Savior?

- What if all signs point to fulfilled Scriptural prophesy and the rapture?

- What if you were to die today?

- What if, what if, what if..........................?

Talk about being a terror victim of *what if*, you should be now after reading all of those. Just think, that only scratches the surface of the fearful *what if* possibilities. I am sure you could add to that list if you have been a victim of *what if*.

Could you prioritize your *what ifs*? Go ahead. List your top three *what ifs* that keep you awake or cause you to lose concentration during the day.

1.

2.

3.

In order to elaborate on some of the *what ifs* I've listed, I will combine some that are related into a few chapters to briefly describe them and how we can choose to win or find peace over them.

You may be thinking that you cannot deal with all of those *what if* chapters, a valid point. Allow me to suggest a couple of approaches for those of you who need the terrorist taken hostage before you read further. One solution would be to pray for God to give you peace over your top 3 *what ifs* you just listed. Pray each day about them. Give them to God every day (maybe several times a day) and when He has freed you from them, read on. When you pray, pray in Jesus' name. Jesus told his disciples,

> Until now you have not asked for anything in my name.
> Ask and you will receive, and your joy will be complete.
> — John 16:24

There is power in prayer when you ask in Jesus' name. There is even more power when 2 or 3 gather in Jesus' name and pray without doubting.

You can be set free, yes, win over the *what ifs* that have terrorized you. Another practical solution that I have used for years comes from my deceased father-in-law, Harold Jones. Dad told me one time when we were having a discussion while I was helping him on a project how he handled worrisome thoughts or troubling situations. He said, "Bob, each night before I go to sleep I imagine a 50 gallon trash barrel sitting next to the head of my bed. Each night I sit on the edge of my bed and one by one mentally, emotionally, and even spiritually deposit all those troubling things into the trash barrel. Then I put a lid on the barrel by praying *God, here they are, I give them to you. Please help me not to go in after them tonight, but allow me to sleep.*" Dad gave me some of the best advice regarding my *what ifs* as a new Christian when I was 22 years old...Don't go dumpster diving to retrieve what you give to God in Jesus' name! Keep the lid closed. So, I pass that along to anyone being terrorized by *what ifs*. It works...prayer, the power of Jesus' name, and choosing consciously to put your *what ifs* in the trash (leaving the lid on them). If you follow through and practice what you have just learned, you will sleep at night. You will have peace that you haven't known.

God wants you to live fearlessly with His peace, free from all the *ifs* and *what ifs* that have kept you sleepless. Psalm 146:7c says, "The Lord sets prisoners free."

Jesus said,

> If you hold to my teachings, you really are my disciples. Then you will know the truth, and the truth will set you free.
> — John 8:31b-32

When you have the Lord "you will not fear the terror of the night." (Psalm 91:5a)

So do not fear *(your "ifs," "what ifs," or "if onlys")*, for I am with you; do not be dismayed, for I am your God. I will strengthen you and help you. I will uphold you with my righteous right hand.

— Isaiah 41:10

Jesus tells us in 1 John 4:18, "There is no fear in love, but perfect love drives out fear...." Great news for those who have allowed the *ifs*, *what ifs*, and *if onlys* to terrorize them. You can be free and face your *if* in life. Ask God for the greatest gift, love (His in your heart) and begin to give love to God, to others, and even to yourself.

- 4 -

Toxic *What Ifs*

The toxicity of a poisoned thought life will produce some of these *what ifs*:

- What if I fail?

- What if I have no purpose?

- What if I cannot face responsibility?

- What if I lose everything?

The hazardous thoughts of these *what ifs* can poison your mind and heart so that your very life seems like a hopeless, toxic dump. To find living cells that contain uncontaminated hope is an enormous challenge. With God's help let's begin to clean up your toxic thinking, starting with "what if I fail."

If you haven't heard, failure does not have to be final! If life is a race, it is certainly a marathon with obstacles that could trip you up, or cause you to fall. But a fall does not mean you are a failure unless you never get up. If you have been tripped up (failed), you can get up and finish the marathon. The Bible records different people's failures and what God's response was. If you are worried about failing, think about David in the Old Testament and Peter in the New Testament. Here are two Biblical examples who failed but did not remain failures.

From David's first introduction as the youngest son of Jesse's eight boys, one can only imagine the *ifs* that were going through his young shepherd's mind. Imagine being called in from watching the flock to stand before the revered and intimidating man of God, Samuel. Then to watch Samuel arise, walk toward David and anoint him to be the King of Israel to replace Saul. Only to have the Lord's Spirit come upon David in power (1 Samuel 16:13) which would have created some *what if* thinking in David. David's story gets more involved as he enters Saul's service, to soothe Saul by playing the harp for him. From harp player to brave warrior—defeating the intimidating giant Goliath with a stone to the forehead as Israel's army and David's brothers watched in fear—you know, even in David's successes there were *ifs* and *what ifs*. Let's fast forward through some of David's life. He has been on quite a winning streak. He has survived assassination attempts, been made King, defeated many armies, and was held in high esteem by the people of Israel. They knew God was with him. But from all the successes comes the *what if* to trip David up. See if you hear it in these words from the Bible from 2 Samuel 11.

> In the spring, at the time when Kings go off to war, David sent Joab out with the King's men and the whole Israelite army. They destroyed the Ammonites and besieged Rabbah. But David remained in Jerusalem.

The first *what if* of this story….. *what if* I stay home and don't go to lead in these battles? Or *what if* I do not do what is expected of me in my job as King, but do something for me?

> One evening David got up from his bed and walked around on the roof of the palace. From the roof he saw a woman bathing. The woman was very beautiful, and David sent someone to find out about her. The man said, "Isn't this Bathsheba, the daughter of Eliam and the wife of Uriah the Hittite?"

Did David hear this? Was he conscious? You see, David had already played the *what if* game in his mind where lust ruled. The risk of *what if* she was married was dismissed because David wanted her. He had made his choice!

> Then David sent messengers to get her. *(Note: messengers!)* She came to him, and he slept with her. Then she went back home. *(Hold on, David. Your failure is going to get more complex.)* The woman conceived and sent word to David saying, "I am pregnant." So David sent this word to Joab: "Send me Uriah the Hittite". When Uriah came to him, David asked him how Joab was, how the soldiers were and how the war was going. Then David said to Uriah, "Go down to your house and wash your feet." So Uriah left the palace, and a gift from the king was sent after him. But Uriah slept at the entrance to the palace with all his master's servants and did not go down to his house. *(Nice try, David, but when you have caved into the temptation of what if that leads to failure, you cannot cover it up.)* When David was told "Uriah did not go home," he asked him, "haven't you just come a distance? Why didn't you go home?" Uriah said to David, "the ark and Israel and Judah are staying in tents, and my master Joab and my lord's men are camped in open fields. How could I go to my house to eat and drink and lie with my wife? As surely as I live, I will not do such a thing!" Then David said to him, "stay here one more day, and tomorrow I will send you back." So Uriah remained in Jerusalem that day and the next. At David's invitation he ate and drank with him, and David made him drunk. But in the evening Uriah went out to sleep on his mat among his master's servants; he did not go home.
> — 2 Samuel 11:1-19

David's *what if* I get him drunk cover up scheme didn't work either.

We see David's failure to go to war as King. We see David's flesh giving in to the failure of adultery with Bathsheba. Hold on, it gets worse as David plans how to make a cover up work so that the people won't find out about their King's failure. This *what if* of sending Uriah back with a sealed letter for him to give Joab, puts David in the pre-meditated murderer category. The letter to Joab said,

> Put Uriah in the front line where the fighting is fiercest. *(Now, watch this.)* Then withdraw from him so he will be struck down and die.
> — 2 Samuel 11:15

David's failures with *what if* keep compounding as he gets the word from Joab that Uriah has died…premeditated murderer is now one more failure title on David's conscience. It looks like the cover up has worked but David of all people should know "your sins will find you out" (Numbers 32:23b). He saw that first hand with King Saul before David became King of Israel. How quickly we forget and our choices become clouded by desire, or instant gratification. How commitment to God and obedience will collapse to sinful choices based on selfish motives. David failed. He chose not to lead his army to battle. He chose not to turn away from lust. He chose to commit adultery. He chose to try to cover up Bathsheba's pregnancy. He chose to be a premeditated murderer. He brought Bathsheba to his house after her time of mourning and made her his wife. She bore him a son. "But the things David had done displeased the Lord." (2 Samuel 11:27b)

From all David's successes now to these sinful failures comes the Lord's man, Nathan, to confront David. David hears Nathan's story about the rich man and the poor man and the rich man taking the poor man's lamb. The Bible says, "David burned with anger against the rich man" (2 Samuel

12:5a), and David said the rich "man deserves to die! He must pay for the lamb four times over, because he did such a thing and had no pity." Then Nathan said to David, (remember your sins will find you out), "You are the man! This is what the Lord, the God of Israel says: *I anointed you King over Israel and delivered you from the hand of Saul. I gave you....and if all this had been too little, I would have given you even more. Why did you despise the word of the Lord by doing evil in his eyes?*" (2 Samuel 12:7-9a)

Talk about God confronting sinful choices that led someone to failure, David was face to face with his *what if* choices that led to David's sins. David is told he will reap calamity in his own household. If you want to know more about what happened to King David's family, you can read on in 2 Samuel 12:11 and the following verses and chapters.

So King David failed miserably because of his bad *what if* choices. David starts to make good choices by confessing, but we tend to forget there are consequences to sinful choices. Even though David confessed that he had sinned against the Lord, even though David pleaded with God to spare the boy Bathsheba had born by David, the boy became ill and died. David comforted Bathsheba. David chooses to lead his army. He starts to fulfill his responsibilities. Yet his family is a mess, (remember out of David's household would come calamity) but let's fast forward to see King David face to face with his "if only" as he mourns over the loss of his son, Absalom. (2 Samuel 18:33) In chapter 19 of 2 Samuel, David's trusted commander Joab hits David with "if you don't go out, not a man will be left with you by nightfall. This will be worse than all the calamities that have come upon you from your youth till now." So David is face to face with another big *what if*. My point in all of this is we can be tempted to make bad, even sinful choices by *what if* and fail miserably. Or we can make good choices with God's help when we are face to face with "what if." When we make good choices, we succeed. But let's say we have failed. Look at what the Bible says about David. It says, "David was a man after God's own heart." (Acts 13:22c) Up until this point, King David has played the *what if* game and failed, but we do know the whole story. He confessed, started making good choices, and was used mightily by God.

Our New Testament candidate for us to study his *what if* choices is Peter. We get our first introduction to Peter when Jesus is walking by the Sea of Galilee and he sees two fisherman brothers, Simon called Peter and Andrew. They are casting nets to catch fish. Jesus calls out to them, "Come, follow me, and I will make you fishers of men." (Matthew 4:19) Allow me to start with this calling of Peter to be a Christ-follower, insert some of Peter's possible "what ifs," and walk you through his failures that we are aware of, so that you can see how he finishes successfully. What amazes me is what the Bible says in Matthew 4:20 about Peter's and Andrew's response to be fishers of men by following Jesus. It says, "at once they left their nets and followed him." Wow! It doesn't sound like there was discussion or debate or even an initial *what if*. Our first picture of Peter is, he will be impetuous and we see more of that from him at other times in the Bible. Impetuous can be good if the choice is good, plus you don't lose time thinking about "what if." But if the choice is bad, look out because you will face *what if* from a different perspective.

One of the impetuous times was when Jesus was preparing His disciples for his death and resurrection. Jesus had asked "who do the people say the Son of Man is?" The disciples gave answers. Then Jesus said, "But what about you, who do you say I am?" (Matthew 16:15) Peter responds with "you are the Christ, the Son of the living God." Jesus replied, "Blessed are you, Simon son of Jonah, for this was not revealed to you by man, but by my Father in Heaven. And I tell you that you are Peter, and on this rock (meaning Peter) I will build my church, and the gates of Hades will not overcome it." (Matthew 16:16-18)

What a picture of Peter, the Rock who was going to be entrusted to lead and build the church after the Lord's departure. Now watch Peter get caught in the *what if* game and hear what Jesus has to say to him. Jesus continues preparing the disciples, letting them know they will be given the keys to the Kingdom of Heaven, that He will have to be killed, but on the third day He will be raised to life. Peter, who has just been called the Rock and given his purpose in life by Jesus, takes Jesus aside. Peter's mind has been in overdrive with *what if* this really happens, that Jesus is killed.

> So Peter began to rebuke Jesus by saying "Never Lord! This shall never happen to you!"
>
> Jesus turned and said to Peter (now this is the same Peter who was just called the Rock and the one whose purpose was to build the church), "Get behind me Satan! You are a stumbling block to me; you do not have in mind the things of God, but the things of men." Then Jesus said to his disciples, "If anyone would come after me, be must deny himself and take up his cross and follow me. For whoever wants to save his life will lose it, and whoever loses his life for me will find it. What good will it be for a man if he gains the whole world, yet forfeits his soul?"
> — Matthew 16:22-6

Peter's *what ifs* were being addressed by Jesus. "What if" you do die, Jesus —what happens to us, to this movement, to the whole Messiah earthly Kingdom thing? "What if" we left the fishing business to follow you and we lose our leader? "What if," "What if," and Jesus said "get behind me Satan." Peter wasn't thinking about the good *what if* possibilities. You cannot be too hard on Peter here because what Jesus was explaining was beyond Peter's earthly (worldly or normal) way of thinking. "Heavenly

Kingdom," "be the Rock," "build the church," were like foreign languages to the impetuous fisherman.

Now the learning to face the *if* in life continues for Peter as Jesus takes Peter, James, and John to the high mountain top. Remember it has just been six days since Peter was put in his place with "get behind me Satan." The Lord had some educating to do for Peter to become the Rock and fulfill his life purpose. So there was Jesus on the mountain top and the Bible says; he was "transfigured before them. His face shone like the sun, and his clothes became as white as the light. Just then there appeared before them Moses and Elijah, talking with Jesus." (Matthew 17:2-3) Can you see some of Peter's *what ifs* being answered in this educational experience? But Peter is still impetuous Peter and he says to Jesus (awesome, cool, wow—sorry, I couldn't resist), "Lord it is good for us to be here. IF you wish, (notice the careful tact Peter is displaying) I will put up three shelters—one for you, one for Moses, and one for Elijah." (Matthew 17:4) Give Peter credit for trying. He liked this mountain top, Heavenly Kingdom experience and if they could stay there with the Lord they wouldn't have to face the other *what ifs* that Peter's mind conjured up out of Jesus' previous teachings. You know, be killed and raised to life again. Good try, Peter! But Peter hears a voice from a bright cloud that enveloped them, "This is my Son, whom I love; with him I am well pleased. Listen to Him!" I always liked the John Wayne line, "Listen up, pilgrim." God was telling Peter, James and John "Listen up." They needed to get it—this is God's Son, this is eternal business and Heaven or Hell hangs in the balance for mankind.

Peter still has a lot to learn as we see him fail in the garden when he takes his sword and cuts off the ear of the servant of the high priest (see Matthew 26:51) only to have Jesus put the ear back on the servant and tell Peter to put his sword away. Moments earlier Peter had told Jesus, "Even if all fall away on account of you, I never will." "I tell you the truth," Jesus answered, "This very night, before the rooster crows, you will disown me three times." But Peter declared, "Even if I have to die with you, I will never disown you." (Matthew 26:32-35a)

Peter, a man's man, the rugged fisherman, Mr. Impetuous, who thinks he has settled his *what ifs* is about to see himself as a failure after all his boisterous commitments. Of course the other disciples chimed in with their commitments to die like Peter. They would not fail Jesus either! Really?

Jesus has just dealt one more time with the *if* in life that He was facing, "if it is possible, may this cup be taken from me. (He is talking about His death on the cross as the atonement for all our sins.) Yet not as I will, but as you will." (Matthew 26:39b) Fast forward a few hours as Jesus has been taken away (the committed disciples had already scattered afraid for their own lives). The high priest wants his charge answered, his *if*: "Tell us if you are the Christ, the Son of God." (Matthew 26:63c)

By the way, where is Peter?

> Now Peter was sitting out in the courtyard, and a servant girl came to him. "You also were with Jesus of Galilee," she said.
>
> But he denied it (that is once) before them all. "I don't know what you're talking about," Peter said.
>
> Then he went out to the gateway, where another girl saw him and said to the people there, "This fellow was with Jesus of Nazareth."
>
> He denied it again, (that's twice) with an oath: "I don't know the man!" (Save your own skin, Peter.)

After a little while, those standing there went up to Peter and said, "Surely you are one of them, for your accent gives you away."

Then he began to call down curses on himself (so much for the Rock) and he swore to them, "I don't know the man!" Immediately a rooster crowed. Then Peter remembered the word Jesus had spoken: "Before the rooster crows, you will disown me three times." And he went outside and wept bitterly.

— Matthew 26:69-75

The failure of Peter in dealing with *what if.*

Good news! Jesus did say He would be resurrected on the 3rd day and He was. Jesus did say Peter would lead the building of Christ's bride, so let's take one more look Biblically at how one who failed miserably with *what if* can become an overcomer, a winner.

Jesus has been resurrected. He is appearing to followers and others so that faith and belief in Him will grow and lessons will be learned for a Christ-follower's life. Jesus finds His disciples fishing, and gives them instructions to throw their nets over the right side of the boat if they want to catch fish. They do and the nets are so full of fish they were unable to haul them in. At this time John says to Peter "it is the Lord." Peter jumps into the water and heads toward Jesus. Like David going to God in confession, Peter goes toward Jesus. They eat. Then Jesus begins the reinstatement process so that Peter can be the Rock.

Jesus said to Peter, "Simon son of John, do you truly love me more than these?"

"Yes Lord," he said, "you know that I love you."

Jesus said, "Feed my lambs."

Again Jesus said, "Simon son of John, do you truly love me?"

He answered, "Yes, Lord, you know that I love you."

Jesus said, "Take care of my sheep."

The third time he said to Peter, "Simon son of John, do you love me?"

Peter was hurt because Jesus asked him a third time, "Do you love me?" He said, "Lord, you know all things; you know that I love you."

Jesus said, "Feed my sheep."

— John 21:15-17

There are a few things here that Jesus was doing and saying to Peter to help Peter become the Rock, the church builder, the overcomer from *what if* failures. First of all, there is the significance of asking Peter three times if Peter loved Jesus (truly, wholeheartedly loved Jesus). Remember Peter denied Jesus three times so to affirm that he loves Him three times carries powerful symbolism when it comes to human healing and restoration. But even more important is getting the Rock to be ready to build and lead the church. The three responses of Jesus are vital to foster Peter's life purpose as he follows Jesus. Jesus said: "Feed my lambs." "Take care of my sheep." "Feed my sheep."

Every pastor, minister, priest would do well to heed what Jesus said to Peter. Here is your ministry mission statement: "Feed the lambs. Take care of my sheep. Feed my sheep." This is what is missing in most 21st century churches today regardless of their size. Does that really need to be interpreted? Baby Christ-followers, growing Christ-followers, and maturing Christ-followers all need care and spiritual food.

Jesus' instructions continue with "Do not leave Jerusalem, but wait for the gift my Father promised, which you have heard me speak about. For John baptized with water, but in a few days you will be baptized with the Holy Spirit." (Acts 1:4b-5)

Peter experiences Pentecost. Peter is now filled with the Holy Spirit. He is no longer the failure who talked big but didn't walk the walk. He is an overcomer, free from the trap of *what if.* Peter preaches his first sermon to fellow Jews citing the prophet Joel: "In the last days, God says, I will pour out my Spirit on all people..........And everyone who calls on the name of the Lord will be saved." (Acts 2:17-21) You would need to read for yourself the rest of the sermon from Acts 2:22-40. So the failure is becoming the Rock, the builder of the church because Acts 2:41 says "Those who accepted Peter's message were baptized and about three thousand were added to their number that day." (That surely made a church growth magazine...*An upstart failure preaches and 3,000 join.*)

King David failed. Peter failed. Both found out that despite their failures God loved them. God wanted them. Yes, God even used them for good! God has the cure for the toxic *what if* that says "failed." You may have gotten an "F" on the exam but the class isn't over. "F" doesn't have to be your final grade.

Paul said it this way to Timothy:

IF we died with Him,
We will also live with Him;
If we endure,
We will also reign with Him.
If we disown Him,
He will disown us;
If we are Faithless, *(now catch this)*
He will remain Faithful, for He cannot disown Himself.
— 2 Timothy 2:11-13

As we face the *ifs* in life, let us move away from the toxic *what if* of failure. We can choose to do so in Christ. We can become new people if we choose Christ.

Therefore, if anyone is in Christ, he is a new creation; the old has gone, the new has come!
— 2 Corinthians 5:17

You can leave your failure, or in my case, failures, and become a new person leaving toxic thinking about failure behind.

- 5 -

The Antidote for *What If* Toxicity

When you have been bitten by a rattlesnake the antidote for the poison has to be taken into your system or the probability of death will be very high. The right antidote taken within the required time frame will help you recover. The poison has been neutralized and you live! You know you have been given another opportunity at life and undoubtedly you will make some changes, especially when it comes to your proximity to poisonous snakes.

You have just been given the antidote to toxic thinking regarding your failures. But even more importantly, you have been given the antidote for any toxic thinking:

> Trust God!
> Believe God!
> Give God your poisonous thoughts!

You see....You are His creation! You are a one-of-a-kind creation. You have a specific, unique purpose for your life. You can find that purpose, and not be in fear of responsibility, or possible loss.

It is important to know *if* you have been poisoned (snake-bitten) and if you want to live, to receive the antidote. What is toxic? Anything containing poisonous material capable of causing serious sickness or death. It doesn't take a lot of poison to create a toxic effect. A little bit of toxic thinking will go a long way toward poisoning all brain activity. The Bible says,

> ...don't you know that a little yeast works through the whole batch of dough? Get rid of the old yeast that you may be a new batch without contaminated yeast...
> — 1 Corinthians 5:6-7

Get rid of the poison. We have a spiritual enemy who wants us to lose to toxic thinking. That is one of his ways he destroys us...kills us. "....your enemy the devil prowls around like a roaring lion looking for someone to devour." (1 Peter 5:8) *IF* he can get us thinking from a poisoned position, a toxic thought life, he has us! Good news, we can take the antidote, Christ. When we do, we will find purpose! The *if* in life is no longer an initial toxic journey because it is "filtered" through Jesus, our Savior. Does that mean that with Jesus life will be easy? The apostle Paul answers that question:

> And now, compelled by the Spirit, I am going to Jerusalem, not knowing what will happen to me there. I only know that in every city the Holy Spirit warns me that prison and hardships are facing me. However, I consider my life worth nothing to me, if only I may finish the race and complete the task the Lord Jesus has given me, the task of testifying to the gospel of God's grace.
> — Acts 20:22-24

Paul is saying, I know my purpose! It is to "testify to the gospel of God's grace." He knows there will be uncertainties. He knows he will face hardships. He knows he could even be killed. But because of Jesus and a clear vision (purpose) for his life, Paul will not allow toxic thinking to prevent him from fulfilling his purpose.

You and I can have the same clarity of vision, the same freedom from toxic thinking. It begins by choosing Jesus to live in your heart then we can have the Holy Spirit's leading (prompting) being "compelled" by the Spirit. We can be secure or certain in uncertainty. "I am going to Jerusalem, not knowing what will happen to me there." (Acts 20:22b) Paul says that "prison and hardships" are ahead (Acts 20:23) so resistance is predictable if Christ has freed you from toxic thinking. With Paul we can have clarity of mind, purpose, and heart. But maybe for someone reading this the toxic thought life is you have accomplished all that you set out to do. So your poisoned thinking is complacency, or "I have done it." You may need to hear:

> Disturb us, Lord, when we are too well pleased with ourselves, When our dreams have come true because we have dreamed too little, When we arrived safely because we sailed too close to the shore."
> — Sir Francis Drake

We need to remember

> where there is no vision, the people perish......
> — Proverbs 29:18

As a minister for over 35 years I have often made calls to people in nursing or rest homes, assisted living quarters, etc. The nursing home or rest home has brought me to tears many times because of the hopelessness that sends a depressing, toxic tornado through every recess of my mind. I have definitely identified a few of the stimuli that cause me to go toxic. One is that people are often placed there by family that do not want to care for them. In fairness, they may not be able to take care of their elderly loved ones. The problem is for the majority of people in nursing home care they are forgotten. Even family may only visit once a month or maybe 2 or 3 times a year (Christmas, Easter, a birthday, or?). It is a prevailing sadness that permeates my mind, the picture of adults sitting, laying, and walking the halls with walkers, prisoners to the facility that is caring for them.

But the second and maybe most telling toxic thought is these folks have no purpose! You take purpose away and before too long the will to live is gone. Do not let toxic thinking keep you from knowing your purpose and pursuing it! We all are going to end up somewhere, hopefully not at a nursing home waiting to die. Why not be a person who finishes life's race strong with purpose? You can...with Christ! You can take hold of responsibility for you with the Lord's help. Yes, you can face life with all its *ifs* and be responsible.

If you are a regular church-goer, you may need to deal with toxic religion. We will take a closer look at toxic religion in the chapter on "Facing Unholy Holiness." In addition for being responsible in how you think, you will need to look at the people you spend your time with each day. I would like to look at that a little closer. Your relationships have an influence on how you think and what decisions you make. Therefore, we need to have a clear head about who we choose to hang with and how they influence our thinking.

- 6 -

BFF (Best Friends Forever) Really?

Have you developed your text language or invented some of your own? My grandchildren were the first to enlighten me that in this high tech, ultra warp speed society there are short cut coded languages today. What may be widely known by the masses would need interpreted for my comprehension. For example the text language "LOL" could have meant "liver on life support," you know, dialysis. Who knew it meant "laugh out loud"? Which brings me back to BFF Really?.

In the struggle to be toxic free, we need to consciously address the *what if* regarding best friends or those we spend our time with in regard to their influence on our thinking that affects our decisions and ultimately our actions. Take time to list those closest to you at this moment in your life. If you can, put them in order of time spent together with one getting the greatest amount of your time.

1.

2.

3.

4.

5.

6.

7.

Now, think about their influence on you and how you think about various things. In facing this *if* in your life, put a "+" behind each name based on whether they are positive, optimistic, "can-do" people; and put a "-" behind each name if they are negative, critical, pessimistic, "no-way" people. Is there any impact that you are feeling either from the "+" friends or the "-" friends at this time in your life?

The Bible tells us "do not be misled: bad company corrupts good character." (1 Corinthians 15:33) What if the company you are keeping is infecting, poisoning how you think, even what kind of talk you talk? The Bible also tells us to "avoid godless chatter, because those who indulge in it will become more and more ungodly." It even states that what they are "teaching (talking about) will spread like gangrene." (2 Timothy 2:16-17) Now you know who you have around you and after honest evaluation of each person whether they are a positive influence to you or a toxic influence. What if you decided to stay away from those who are toxic? I am talking about those who are critical regardless of the topic. I am talking about those who are negative and complain, complain, complain. I am talking about those who want to control; you know, those who are overly demanding and verbally abusive. I am talking about those who would try to tempt you to do something your conscience tells your brain isn't right to do. What if you set some perimeters or boundaries for your thinking when you are with these folks? Why do that? You want to get rid of the mind poison that is affecting you. Even Jesus did that when he told Peter,

> Get behind me, Satan! You are a stumbling block to me;
> you do not have in mind the things of God, but the things
> of men.
>
> — Matthew 16:33

You see, your "so-called" friends, your "best friends forever" may not really be best friends who have your good in mind! You may have to say to some of them, "I'm not going there with you." (Be that in a conversation or a physical place.) You may even have to cut off some toxic relationships. Second Corinthians 6:4 tells us to "avoid being unequally yoked." The people of Israel were warned about toxic thinking when they were told (more than once) "do not marry those who follow false gods." (Deut.7) Paul told Timothy in 2 Timothy 3:1-5 about toxic people and that Timothy was to "have nothing to do with them." The Bible has so much instruction regarding our behavior when it comes to toxic relationships. "Do not envy wicked men, do not desire their company." (Proverbs 24:1) Or how about "he who walks with the wise grows wise, but a companion of fools suffers harm." (Proverbs 13:20) "Do not be misled: *bad company corrupts good character*." (1 Corinthians 15:33) We do not need to be tied to toxic relationships that will influence us to choose poisonous *what if* thinking. Clearly we are to "avoid being unequally yoked." (2 Corinthians 6:4)

So if your close friends have iinfluenced you to be "sexting" today, stop the inappropriate behavior. We know from 1 Thessalonians 5:21 and 22, we are to "test everything." We are to "hold on to the good." We are to "avoid every kind of evil." To do that you may need to say "good-bye" to some "BFFs" because they bring influencing toxins to your mind! So the question is good influence or not? Where are you headed? Will you do what is necessary to have pure thoughts and pure motives that will be pleasing to God and constructive for you? Sell out to Jesus and the purity of the gospel. He wants to be your best friend. Jesus is the true BFF!

- 7 -

Facing the Toxic *IF* of Unholy Holiness

People around you can be a spiritual asset or a toxic curse as we have just discussed in the previous chapter. But what if the toxicity is *unholy holiness* in the church or in people professing to be very religious? Having not been raised in a church as a child or teen to say that I was naïve about the church would be a gross understatement. Actually ignorant would even be an understatement. I had not known Jesus as Savior until March, 1965. After 11 years in public education I answered the call to ministry the third week of June, 1979. At that time until the present I have learned a lot about the church, religion, and *unholy holiness.* May I add that I am still learning and astonished at times what is done in the name of Jesus or religion or holiness. History when studied supports what I have just stated. I will always remember a great Christian leader who had pastored for years a very large church in Bethany, Oklahoma and had become the president of Southern Nazarene University saying to me, "Bob, it is amazing, a real miracle the church does as much good as it does." That was Dr. Gilliland's statement to me in 1989 at Tucson, Arizona where I had brought him as our featured guest for a leadership weekend. After all these years his statement, oh so true, still resonates in my soul.

The church can be the *Christ-filled*, compassionate care center offering hope, help, and healing for hurting people. The church in contrast to that can be the meanest, most slanderous, hurtful and even *hate-filled* place anyone could ever experience. Allow me to address what I call *unholy holiness*, and religion in the disguise called the church. First and foremost we must understand that the church is not a building or a form, or a routine religious behavior. The church is people. The true, unadulterated church is the Bride of Christ, the wholly-devoted, heart-surrendered to Jesus followers. These people have one purpose: to be Christ's ambassadors wherever they are, no matter what they are doing. This Bride of Christ has in mind and heart to love God first and to love their neighbors next. They live to pass on the love and hope they have in their faith journey with Jesus. Read chapter 11 of the book of Hebrews to see the kind of faith the true church possess. The Bible says,

> But my righteous one will live by faith. And if he shrinks back I will not be pleased with him.
> — Hebrews 10:38

The true church is shrink proof, as we see in the next verse.

> But we are not of those who shrink back and are destroyed, but of those who believe and are saved.
> — Hebrews 10:39

I could fill a couple of books with actions by people who call themselves the church that were unholy, mean-spirited, evil, hateful, uncaring, even demonstrating pre-meditated behaviors that divided churches, families, and marriages. Character assassinations are a common tool used by these folks. Accusations flow from whispered rumors to those rumors carefully clothed in the name of prayer concerns about someone. We need to be wise when this kind of toxic *unholy holiness* is being passed on to us. We need to see it for what it is—an attack by the enemy of our soul. He has one agenda: to steal, kill, and destroy a person from having faith in God through Jesus Christ our Savior. Jesus tells us Satan's agenda in John 10:10. "The thief (Satan) comes only to steal and kill and destroy; I have come that they may have life, and have it to the full." Therein lies the difference between those operating as the church, the *unholy holiness* crowd versus the real Bride of Christ. One crowd is out to destroy through accusations, innuendos, in the name of concern (so pray for . . . . .), while the Christ-follower gives grace and hope through Jesus.

I have seen the ugly, *unholy holiness* crowd drive new converts away from worship service times with remarks over the type of clothes a new convert was wearing to "concerned" comments about how they handled their children, to . . . . . (you go ahead and fill in the blank). I've watched and been shocked by unfounded accusations that were only meant to hurt because of envy, comparing, jealousy, etc. I'm reminded that Satan is the "accuser of the brethren." (Revelation 12:10) The true Bride of Christ does not bring "...slanderous accusations...." (2 Peter 2:11) Read second Peter to get a description of how the unrighteous, the unholy treat others. It is a very vivid description of how those behave who pretend to be the church or pretend to be religious. Their sinful nature is in control of them and they are so "self-focused" they do not care about the victim they are destroying. The victim suffers the hurt of character assassination and destroyed reputation. The Bible also tells us,

> If anyone.....does not keep a tight rein on his tongue, he
> deceives himself and his religion is worthless.
> — James 1:26

So how do you recognize these impostors? Before I answer that please remember this analogy, not every animal that enters a barn is a purebred milk cow. Goats, pigs, horses, donkeys, cats, dogs, even chickens sometimes get in the barn. Watch out for the goats! As I stated, they level slanderous accusations, they also come across as very religious. (I'm talking pious or devout). They are the modern day Pharisees—the crowd that is better than everyone else. No one measures up to their standards. That is the clue because their standards are based on the externals. Their religion is all about self and works and how it looks, not about the heart. The Bride of Christ has the heart of Christ not the selfish heart. The third clue regarding the religious, unholy crowd hiding behind the name church is they pervert the gospel. The Bible even talks about them.

> I am astonished that you are so quickly deserting the one who called you by the grace of Christ and are turning to a different gospel—which is really no gospel at all. Evidently some people are throwing you into confusion and are trying to pervert the gospel of Christ.
> — Galatians 1:6-7

That is exactly what the religious, unholy crowd does. They try to pervert, corrupt, distort and poison the true church. Like the Pharisees they are all about *the look* of church. Their pride is in *showing off* but the Bible gives this clear warning:

> Woe to you, teachers of the law and Pharisees, (with their 613 additional commands) you hypocrites! You clean the outside of the cup and dish, but inside they are full of greed and self-indulgence.
> — Matthew 23:25

To the religious unholy crowd pretending to be holy,

> ....no one will be declared righteous....by observing the law; rather, through the law we become conscious of sin.
> — Romans 3:20

The law shows us our need for a Savior. We do not do works to earn God's acceptance. We do good because we have been accepted, saved by Jesus. Therefore out of our love for Jesus, we do good deeds. As Bill Hybels has said in defining religion versus Christianity, "Religion is do" and "Christianity is done." The righteousness the Bride of Christ has

> ...comes through faith in Jesus Christ to all who believe.
> — Romans 3:22

You can face the toxic *what if* that comes from the religious or *unholy holiness* crowd. You do it by knowing what God's Word says and remembering Jesus' mission was to save, not destroy. You can do it by being certain you personally have surrendered or sold out to the purity of the gospel where grace, love, and peace abound. You can win by having an up-to-date relationship with Jesus and not a religious ritual. Are you a good influence, a real picture of the Bride of Christ? You can be! You can be holy (set apart by God) and not be a Pharisee in the 21st century. With Christ you are His ambassador, His masterpiece, created to do the good God has planned.

> God saved you by His grace when you believed. And you can't take credit for this; it is a gift from God. Salvation is not a reward for the good things we have done, so none of us can boast about it. For we are God's masterpiece, He has created us anew in Christ Jesus, so we can do the good things he planned for us long ago.
> — Ephesians 2:8-10

Created for a purpose. Think on that as you say so long to the toxic effects of religion and *unholy holiness*. Look at *what if* God wanted you to . . . . . Go ahead and ask Him to fill in the blank with you.

- 8 -

What If You Have Been a Victim

Victims vary in age, in gender, in degrees of atrocities that they may have suffered. The hard truth to apply if received (there is that pesky two letter word *if* again) is that there is a time that eventually comes where the victim becomes a volunteer. To overcome being a victim each person has to consciously and prayerfully decide that enough is enough. That being a volunteer for more is not going to be allowed. Facing the thought, "*what if* I've become a volunteer for more suffering," will take honesty and courage. "Lord, I pray right now for the person who will read this chapter who has been victimized, that You will heal them, set them free from this terrible *what if* so that they will not end up a volunteer for more pain!" Amen and Amen!

When I think of abuse, many people flash through my mind. From young children, to teens, to adults, the real people and their accounts of abuse flood my very being. You see I was a public educator/administrator for eleven years and during that time I moonlighted as a deputy sheriff for almost nine of those years. Add those years with over 34 years of ministry and the real stories I have been told, some I actually witnessed, are almost unbelievable. It is hard to comprehend how one person can so abuse another. Yet as we know all too well, it happens! Our world is filled with victims of abuse. So if you have been abused, if you are a victim, you may be thinking you are the only one. The truth is no matter what kind of abuse you have been a victim of, there are others in the world who know your pain. Some of the abusive stories I have heard as a pastor, policeman, and public educator include: physical beatings, sexual abuse, being sold by a parent to be a prostitute, being forced into some form of slavery for money for a parent, being traded to do sexual favors for a husband's extra income, forced into the pornographic industry by an adult, etc. Two sisters age 5 and 7 will always live in my mind. They were victims of their grandfather's sexual fantasies. As the grandfather confessed his incest with these two little girls, I (as a father of 3 daughters) wanted to jump over my pastoral desk and use him to rearrange my office and while I was at it rearrange his face. Pastors may have to listen to some of this, but I wish God would release us to inflict some physical pain on those who victimize, especially those who victimize children. Unfortunately or maybe fortunately, God didn't give me that privilege.

Another vivid memory is of a family of four children. The oldest was 15 and she had been one of my students. This memory is also very real for me. I was moonlighting (working an extra job) as a deputy when I received a call to back up my shift sergeant at a domestic problem. When I arrived the sergeant was on the scene with his squad car pulled across the yard in front of the front door of the residence. The sergeant, with gun drawn in one hand, was taking cover behind the open squad car door. He instructed me to go to the side door and on his "go," we would both enter. He would go through the front door and I would enter through the side door. The county sheriff's dispatcher had told us a frantic child had called and said "we need help. Dad is beating us and he said he was going to kill our big sister" (the girl I had taught as a student). I could see the Dad. He was a huge man. His double-barrel shotgun lay on the coffee table behind him. When the sergeant had arrived, he saw the dad waving the shotgun around and gesturing. As we entered, I grabbed the shotgun and removed the shells. The sergeant confronted the dad. You could feel the fear in the room. As I looked at the kids, I could see swollen eyes from being punched, bloody noses, cut lips, etc. They were huddled in the corner on their knees with their 15 year old big sister draped over them trying to hold them all close. Meanwhile, the dad is verbally victimizing anyone who would listen with his comments about the kids and that they would pay for calling the "pigs." I found myself picking up this burly 350 plus pounder by his hairy armpits and pressing him hard against the wall (a few times) as my sergeant said, "I'll cuff him and take him. You help the kids." Really what he was saying was, "don't be stupid and add to his list of victims; help the kids." He was right! With four badly beaten kids on the floor in the corner, this moonlight sheriff's deputy didn't need to be victim number five. You see, the dad's goading me along with the real picture of hurt kids almost led me to volunteer to be victim number five. There are lots of other true stories I could share but this chapter is about helping victims and making sure they haven't become volunteers for more pain.

There are various victims in the Bible. I would like us to focus on one, Joseph, and look closely at this victim's story and how he kept from being a volunteer for more suffering. If you want the whole story of Joseph's birth, you would need to start reading the Bible in Genesis where God remembers Rachel's plea for a child and she gives birth to Joseph. (Genesis 30:23-24) Jacob, Joseph's father, had several children by Leah and Rachel (his wives) and their maidservants, Bilhah and Zilpah. Altogether Jacob had twelve sons. Now for our victim's story.

> Joseph, a young man of seventeen, was tending the flocks
> with his brothers, the sons of Bilhah and the sons of
> Zilpah, his father's wives, and he brought their father

a bad report about them. Now Israel (God had changed his name from Jacob) loved Joseph more than any of his other sons because he had been born to him in his old age; and he made a richly ornamented robe for him. When his brothers saw that their father loved him more than any of them, they hated him and could not speak a kind word to him. Joseph had a dream, and when he told it to his brothers, they hated him all the more. He said to them, *Listen to this dream I had: We were binding sheaves of grain out in the field when suddenly my sheaf rose upright, while your sheaves gathered around mine and bowed down to it.* (You might think Joseph, our soon to be victim, isn't very smart since he already knows his brothers are jealous of him.) His brothers said to him, *Do you intend to reign over us? Will you actually rule us?* And they hated him all the more because of his dream and what he said.

— Genesis 37:2-8

While one dream wasn't enough to build the hostility, he has another dream with the "sun and moon and eleven stars" bowing down to him. So he not only tells his brothers but his father, who responds with "will your mother and I and your brothers actually bow down to the ground before you?" (Genesis 37:10b)

So Joseph is sent to check on his brothers by Israel and when they saw him from a distance coming toward them, the brothers made their plans to kill him. But one of the brothers, Reuben persuaded them not to kill him. Instead they stripped him of his robe and threw him into a cistern. While Joseph is down in this empty cistern his brothers see the Ishmaelites coming and Judah convinces the rest of them to sell Joseph to them. Joseph, the victim of his brothers, went from being left to die in the cistern to being sold into slavery. You know he already had some painful emotional scars. The Ishmaelites bought Joseph for 20 shekels of silver (about 8 ounces) and took him to Egypt. The brothers complete the cover up to their father by presenting Joseph's goat-blood dipped robe to him. Israel mourned for Joseph and refused to be comforted because he believed some ferocious animal had eaten him. (See Genesis 37:31-33) The victim's story is far from over as Joseph is sold "in Egypt to Potiphar, one of Pharaoh's officials, the captain of the guard." (Genesis 37:36) Joseph, the victim, is just beginning to be indoctrinated into further pain. He is not volunteering for more, but this victim is going to get more.

We pick up the story of Joseph again in Genesis 39. Remember, Joseph is a slave in Potiphar's household. The Bible says,

> The Lord was with Joseph (even though he was a victim) and he prospered, and he lived in the house of his Egyptian master. When his master saw that the Lord was with him (Joseph had to be doing something right in his victim status) and that the Lord gave him success in everything he did. Joseph found favor in his eyes and became his attendant. Potiphar put Joseph in charge of his household and he entrusted him to his care of everything he owned.
> — Genesis 39:2-4

Potiphar was being blessed through Joseph and it says, "With Joseph in charge, Potiphar did not concern himself with anything except the food he ate." (Genesis 39:6b)

But the victim, Joseph, is about to be victimized again. Potiphar's wife wanted Joseph. But Joseph refuses her. "Come to bed with me" and he says, "No." But one day when none of the other servants were in the house, after days of trying to seduce Joseph, she grabbed his cloak and said, "Come to bed with me!" But this time Joseph ran out of the house, while she still had his cloak. She called for her servants, and falsely accused Joseph. "Look....he left his cloak beside me and ran out of the house!" (Genesis 39:12b-15) When Potiphar hears his wife's story, "he burned with anger." Potiphar had Joseph put in prison where the king's prisoners were confined. Once again, Joseph was a victim!

> But while Joseph was there in the prison, the Lord was with him; (even though you have been victimized it doesn't mean the Lord isn't with you or that He has forgotten you) the Lord showed Joseph kindness and granted him favor in the eyes of the prison warden. So the warden put Joseph in charge of all those held in the prison, and Joseph was made responsible for all that was done there....the Lord gave Joseph success in whatever he did.
>
> — Genesis 39:21-23

Fast forward to Joseph interpreting the King's cup-bearer and baker's dreams, setting the stage for the victim to be the interpreter of Pharaoh's dream. This interpretation of the seven years of coming famine that would ravage the land, landed Joseph, the victim, the position of second-in-command. From being hated by his brothers, to a cistern to die, to being sold twice as a slave, to being falsely accused by Potiphar's wife and imprisoned, to second-in-command. Can you see what God can do for a victim? He can do it for you too. But Joseph's story isn't over; it is just getting to the good part. Remember the sheaves, the sun, & the moon bowing down?

The famine had spread over the whole country but Joseph had Egyptian storehouses built and filled with grain.

So Pharaoh told the Egyptians, *Go to Joseph and do what he tells you*.....Joseph opened the storehouses and sold grain to the Egyptians, for the famine was severe throughout Egypt. And all the countries came to Egypt to buy grain from Joseph...

— Genesis 41:55-57

Israel tells his sons, "I have heard that there is grain in Egypt. Go down there and buy some for us, so that we may live and not die." (Genesis 42:2) Here come the 10 sheaves (Joseph's brothers)! Israel "did not send Benjamin, Joseph's brother with the others, because he was afraid that harm might come to him." (Genesis 42:4)

The picture unfolds when Joseph, the second-in-command to Pharaoh, the governor of the land, recognizes his ten brothers immediately as they are bowing to him. Joseph pretends to be a stranger to them as he speaks harshly with this question: "Where do you come from?" "From the land of Canaan," they replied, "to buy food." The brothers did not recognize Joseph. Joseph accuses them of being "spies." "You have come to see where our land is unprotected." Joseph continues to say they are spies despite their explanations of who they are and why they came. Joseph, the victim, has opportunity to get revenge. Joseph wants to see his real full brother, Benjamin. Joseph sets the half-brothers up by "if you are honest men....." then Joseph gave orders to put ½ of each brother's silver back in their sack and then fill them with grain. The great set up has been accomplished. As Israel is told what has happened and the demand from the "man" (Joseph), he responds with ..."everything is against me." Finally after many *ifs* and promises to Israel from his sons, Reuben and Judah, regarding Benjamin's safety, Israel consents to send Benjamin along with the double silver and other gifts for "the man."

Joseph's revenge isn't really revenge at all if you read the full account in Genesis 43, 44 and 45. It is a great set up for his plan to get to keep Benjamin. Finally, after hearing Judah's story about his father Israel with all the *ifs* of life, Joseph is left alone with his brothers and at that time he said to them, "I am Joseph." (Genesis 45:3a) Can you imagine what was going through the brother's heads? Fear, terror, and probably "we are dead!"

> I am your brother Joseph, the one you sold into Egypt! And now, do not be distressed (Joseph is no longer going to be the victim) and do not be angry with yourselves for selling me here, because it was to save lives that God sent me ahead of you. (That is what happens when a victim is able to help other victims, lives are saved.)....to preserve for you a remnant on earth to save your lives by a great deliverance.
>
> — Genesis 45:46-7

Joseph gives his brothers orders to go get their father, their families, etc. and come to live under his care. They do, but they were still dealing with the guilt of what they had done to Joseph. Now we can see Joseph is no longer the captive victim, but his brothers are the ones being victimized. This was especially true after Israel died. "They said, *what if (there it is...the haunting phrase for victims) Joseph holds a grudge against us and pays us back for all the wrongs we did to him?*" (Genesis 50:15) So they make up a story about their father's last instructions asking Joseph to forgive his brothers' sins against him. The Bible tells us "when their message came to him, Joseph wept." (Genesis 50:17e) They throw themselves down before Joseph (remember the dream from the beginning) saying, "We are your slaves." (Genesis 50:18b)

Now listen to the freed victim, Joseph, who is refusing to volunteer for any more suffering.

> Don't be afraid. Am I in the place of God? You intended
> to harm me, but God intended it for good to accomplish
> what is now being done, the saving of many lives.
> — Genesis 50:19-20

This is one of the greatest stories Biblically about a victim choosing to not be victimized by hate, anger, revenge, pity, etc. That is the powerful message that comes through to all victims, that you do not need to volunteer for more pain. With God you can receive healing. You can be given purpose. Your past pain does not need to keep you imprisoned. Like God told the children of Israel in Isaiah 43:18 and 19a

> Forget the former things; do not dwell on the past. See,
> I am doing a new thing...

Over the years I have witnessed victims be healed, set free from the deep scars of painful pasts. It is a beautiful testimony of what God can do to overcome the evil that has been done to someone.

If we could leave the past in the past, we could go forward with God. Often I have told victims "yesterday ended at midnight," and that the "past has no future." Both are very true statements that can be helpful for healing and leaving the victimized state. It is one of Satan's traps to keep people victimized, especially if you are a follower of Jesus who is focusing on yesterday. We do have to "forget the former things" to go forward. We at least need to let the scars stay scabbed over. Don't pick at the scabs! You can decide today to no longer volunteer for more pain or be a victim of past pain. The choice truly is yours. IF Joseph could leave the victim status and see the big picture, you can too!

- 9 -

Devalued

Whether it was from victimization, *unholy holiness,* or betrayal you know what worthless feels like. How you got to feeling devalued is one subject, but it is not as important as what you choose to do about overcoming devalued. *IF* devalued has led you to feel devastated and desperate, you need to know that with God you can overcome being destroyed. When you are in the deepest day of your devalued disease, *if* you look up, you will find your Defender and Deliverer. You do not have to succumb to or live in the devil's devalued "d's": desperation, destruction, devastation, etc. He uses those to rob you of peace, joy, and an overcomer's mind set. He will try to make you double-minded, distressed, dismayed, divided, and disgraced with the result being, you will feel worthless, a failure, and physically/spiritually/mentally/emotionally drained. When we deal with devalued, we are often deceived by the devil and self! We might be in the midst of despair like King David was when he wrote this Psalm.

> Save me, O God,
> For the waters have come up to my neck.
> I sink in the miry depths (of the devalued—my input),
> where there is no foothold,
> I have come into the deep waters;
> The floods (all the "d's" just mentioned with devalued)
> engulf me.
> I am worn out calling for help;

My throat is parched.
My eyes fail, looking for my God.

Those who hate me without reason outnumber the hairs
on my head;
Many are my enemies without cause,
Those who seek to destroy me.
I am forced to restore what I did not steal.

— Psalm 69:1-4

What a description of the feelings of one who has been devalued! David knows God as a holy God who "defends" (Psalm 68:5) and "delivers" (Psalm 18:2, 40:17, 140:7, 144:2 and 37:40). For us to leave the desert of the devalued, we need the Defender and Deliverer. We do not need to try to defend or deliver ourselves from this desolate state of being devalued. We do not need to deride ourselves and derail what God wants to do for us. Isaiah the prophet, prophesying against Babylon describes "an invader who comes from the desert, from a land of terror." His vision describes how the devil comes to us when we have been devalued. "The traitor betrays, the looter loots." Isaiah goes on to say, "I am staggered by what I hear, I am bewildered by what I see. My heart falters, fear makes me tremble;..." (Isaiah 21:1, 2, 3b & 4a) That is how we feel when we have been devalued.

Regardless of who or how many are devaluing you, regardless of the amount of untruth being told about you, the Defender does defend! The Deliverer does deliver! God takes our desert and can make it into an oasis. God takes our mess, (everything that involves you and feeling devalued) and makes His message. You will leave the land of terror, of worthlessness, and with God be an overcomer! No longer will you shrink back or hide. No longer will the *if* connected to devalued thinking keep you defeated. With Jesus, you are an overcomer.

IF God is for us, who can be against us? He who did not spare his own Son, but gave him up for us all—how will he not also, along with him, graciously give us all things? ...Who shall separate us from the love of Christ? Shall trouble or hardship or persecution or famine or nakedness or danger or sword?...No, in all these things we are more than conquerors through Christ who loved us.

— Romans 8:31-32 35 37

You see with Christ you can win over the *if* of devalued!

When someone has lessened your worth, when you have allowed being devalued to dominate your every cell, hear Jesus' words: "...In this world you will have trouble. (You will have to face the *what if* of being devalued) But take heart! I (Jesus) have overcome the world." (John 16:33) We can "demolish arguments and every pretension (anything said or done to devalue us) that sets itself up against the knowledge of God, and we take captive every thought to make it obedient to Christ." (2 Corinthians 10:5) "For though we live in the world, we do not wage war as the world does. The weapons we fight with are not the weapons of the world. On the contrary, they have divine power to demolish strongholds." (2 Corinthians 10:3-4) We need to fight "devalued" and all its *what ifs* with supernatural weapons. God calls us his dear children and says, we "are from God and have overcome the evil ones, because the one who is in you (if you belong to Jesus) is greater than the one who (accuses and devalues) is in the world." (1 John 4:4) We need the faith-based, faith-filled, overcomer attitude that defeats the *what ifs* of devalued!

You are not worthless or of less value. You are a child of the Creator God, who made you in His image. "If our God is greater, if our God is stronger, who can stand (devalue) against us?" We do not need to duck and hide when we have experienced the *what ifs* of being devalued. God did not devalue us. He valued us so much He sent His only Son to die and make a way for us. We need to remember we are of great worth to God. We can overcome devalued and any other persecutions or trouble by "the Blood of the Lamb and our testimony." (See Revelations 12)

Begin by writing down the name or names of those who have devalued you.

1.

2.

3.

4.

5.

6.

Now pray the blood of Christ over you and over each one of them. Give to God exactly how you have been devalued. Ask God to defend you and to deliver you from any effects it is having on you as His child. He is the great Defender and Deliverer. He will empower you to be an overcomer! When you were a child it is possible that you faced some of your feelings of being devalued on the playground (maybe being the last one chosen, cooties are contagious you know, or you were called Tubby or Fatty, etc.). Playgrounds can be life-scarring battlefields where devalue is etched on you for life. Newsflash, you do not have to be a devalued, playground victim! You can be healed. You can say, I am of worth! I am an overcomer and the *what if* of devalued is not welcome in my being nor will it be allowed to take up residence! My prayer would be in the form of this poem I have authored:

Enough
Courage enough to trust...
Faith enough to believe...
Strength enough to choose...
Conscious enough to begin...
Determined enough to be real...
Caring enough to hurt...
Yet, loving enough to forgive!

— Bob Shephard

Say "enough" to being devalued and be an overcomer in Christ.

- 10 -

What If It Smells Like Smoke

Hickory smoke can be an alluring vapor if you love barbecue smoked meats or pecan vapor can also draw in smoked fish lovers. Why a chapter regarding "what if it smells like smoke?" Smoke is defined as a "vaporous matter arising from something burning." My contention is that temptation is smoke, that vaporous appeal to pull you into something that will ultimately cost you more than you could ever have calculated. Smoke may stain you. Smoke can drive the true you out of hiding, like a bee-keeper will "smoke out" bees when necessary. Smoke can keep you from seeing clearly. Here in Oklahoma there are signs on interstates and turnpikes warning you, "DO NOT DRIVE INTO THE SMOKE." That is what this chapter is, a warning: "Don't be drawn into temptation." Recognize the smoke of temptation is a "smoke-screen" to get you to sin. If you have ever been in thick smoke, not only can you not see clearly, but you will have trouble breathing, even thinking clearly. You will even end up smelling like smoke. Your clothes will get saturated and you will stink.

My father was a two to three pack a day cigarette smoker when I was growing up. He used to take me with him on his milk route and livestock runs. There in the cab of his truck the smoke would be so overwhelming for me that I couldn't see clearly. My eyes would burn. My nostrils would fill with his exhaled smoke, and I would get deathly sick. I'd have to make him stop the truck so I could get out and regurgitate. After several years of that I can tell you, I have never smoked nor will I ever. I learned first-hand what "second-hand" smoke could accomplish. In the same way, "second-hand" temptation can cause you to be in a sick stupor, leaving you weak and unable to function. It can make you sick.

This chapter, "If It Smells Like Smoke," is intended to cause you to be conscious of temptation(s) that would separate us from a loving, holy God. To recognize the smoke of Satan's temptational schemes, to face the reality of our choices, and to respond to God's truths regarding temptation, as well as the Holy Spirit's leadership, is the purpose for this chapter. Four words beginning with the letter "R" come to mind when dealing with the smoke of temptation. They are: recognize, reality, responsibility, and resist. If you practice these four "R's", you will know "if it smells like smoke—leave it alone."

Allow me to share a few true stories of people I ministered to over 34 years and the results of how they faced the smoke of temptation. Then I would also like to weave in some Biblical characters who faced the smoke of temptation as well as scripture that tells us what God would want to do.

From the majestic peak of this Bradshaw mountain you could see, on a clear day, the San Francisco peaks in Flagstaff, Arizona—some 120 plus miles away. Nestled in the tall Ponderosa pines and huge boulders on the top of this mountain was an exclusive subdivision. There sat a 4,000 to 5,000 square foot house whose inhabitants I knew very well. A family of five called it "home." They, the couple, were living the American dream with all the amenities they could charge. The three car garage, the long driveway leading up to it lined with all the adult toys that wouldn't fit in the garage told the story. Even children's toys were littered among the adult toys, i.e. A high dollar speed boat, the latest 4-wheel drive jeep, the luxury convertible, the family's SUV, his and her motorcycles, personal water-crafts, kids motorized rides, etc. In addition, the clothes being worn all sported the "right" logos.

As much as it seemed to be the perfect American dream for all involved, the smoldering smoke of temptation's consequences was a lingering presence. The smoke went unnoticed. The inhalation of temptation always winning had the couple in a stupor. The children were clueless except that mom and dad seemed to yell at each other more. The dad had to work harder and longer. He had to take more promotions in order to make minimum payments on the house, the toys, and their out-of-control spending. It just kept getting harder to make even minimum payments. Forty-five hours had become 60 to 65 hours and then 75 to 80 hours a week.

His wife was lonely and met that need by demanding more money/material things. She got a job in a potential career field that could bring in significant money, provided she went along with the demands. After all, why should she be denied? Besides her mother lived nearby and she had volunteered to help with the children. All too soon these childhood sweethearts hardly saw each other, even though they had the same address of residence. Their communication was hardly more than hand-written notes for each other left on a kitchen counter-top or taped to the garage entry door to the house. The children were picked up and dropped off at grandmother's or the daycare. They were welcomed home at night by a neighbor's teen-aged daughter who would get them ready and into bed. Days could go by without them really seeing or talking to mom and dad. Fast food was the daily diet.

You see, the smoke of temptations had such a numbing effect that Jack and Jill (the parents) couldn't see the destruction that was happening to them or their children. Enough was not a familiar vocabulary word for this couple. The temptation of more continued to put a thick haze over their minds, keeping them from recognizing reality.

Unfortunately, I would see this true story repeated many times with various couples in my thirty-five plus years of ministry. Usually the smoke of temptation has to build into a roaring four-alarm fire before people face their problem(s). Too often when the smoke of temptation has become a devastating fire, people turn to a pastor, a counselor, or a close friend for a quick fix or a save. By that time it is often too late, but if both people truly turn to Jesus and want help—miracles happen. There are real people's stories who have been saved, but I do not know of any that were a "quick" fix!

In this case, Jack and Jill fell down off the mountain top, losing everything. Jill kept the three children when she got the divorce. Jack went to work in the North Country on a ranch, tending after livestock, living in a line shack away from civilization for 10 ½ months a year. Jill eventually remarried. The children were in and out of trouble as they grew up. Jill's life ended tragically one spring day. She took her own life as the smoke of temptation's devastation led her to her demise. Temptation's smoke had wreaked havoc with this family of five, and with other family and friends who cared about Jack and Jill. It could have been so different, IF Jack and Jill had recognized the smoke of temptation, IF Jack and Jill had faced the reality of temptation's smoke, IF they would have taken personal and marital responsibility for their choices regarding the smoke of temptation, and IF they would have resisted temptation's smoke with God's help.

Over the years as a pastor, friend, and father, I have shed many tears, felt great pain, and prayed a lot for the many Jack and Jill accounts that were very real to me. The smoke of temptation starting as seemingly innocent, harmless conversations with a co-worker on coffee break that lead to the divorce of two families with all its pain because of affairs. Or the "just one look" at the internet porn-sites that lead to "XXX" addictions, that lead from fantasies to actions, that lead to getting caught ("be sure your sins will find you out" Numbers 32:23), that lead to prison time. Dr. James Dobson, Focus on the Family Founder, stated after serving on President Reagan's commission to gather data against the pornography industry he wished he had never seen some of the images. They troubled him for years. My list of real people who didn't see the smokescreens used by Satan to tempt is very, very long. IF only they would have followed God's Biblical truth when it comes to temptation. IF only they would have done what the Bible says to do in regards to how we are to respond to temptation. So the subtle smoke of undetected temptation will become a reality at some point, hopefully before you are totally asphyxiated. Whether it is the smell of mother's fresh-baked chocolate chip cookies pulling on you to take "just one" as a kid, even though you'd heard mom's "do not eat any cookies." Or the sight of a naked-beauty called Bathsheba from King David's eyes looking down on her from his balcony while she bathed. Or it's okay to "fudge" on your taxes. Or it's only a partially false statement. Or take a 30-minute break instead of the allotted 10 minute break because "everyone else is." Satan's temptations are often presented behind some type of smokescreen connected to an *if* in your everyday life. The *if* is clouded with a temporary reward that sounds so good. Just listen to the *ifs* and temporary rewards thrown at Jesus:

> The tempter came to him and said, "If you are the Son of
> God, tell these stones to become bread."

Jesus answered, "It is written: 'Man shall not live on bread alone, but on every word that comes from the mouth of God.'"

Then the devil took him to the holy city and had him stand on the highest point of the temple. "If you are the Son of God," he said, "throw yourself down. For it is written: " 'He will command his angels concerning you, and they will lift you up in their hands, so that you will not strike your foot against a stone.'"

Jesus answered him, "It is also written: 'Do not put the Lord your God to the test.'"

Again, the devil took him to a very high mountain and showed him all the kingdoms of the world and their splendor. "All this I will give you," he said, "if you will bow down and worship me."

Jesus said to him, "Away from me, Satan! For it is written: 'Worship the Lord your God, and serve him only.'" Then the devil left him, and angels came and attended him.

— Matthew 4:3-11

This powerful passage regarding Jesus' temptation after 40 days of fasting where He is in a physically weakened condition teaches us how to deal with the smoke of temptation: First, it is to see the temptation clearly for what it truly is. Whether it was the smoke of turning stones to bread, or the smoke of you cannot get hurt, go ahead do it, or the smoke of temporary power/material wealth if you would just worship someone or something other than God. Clearly seeing the temptation is a must and that comes by knowing God's truths from the Bible (not just partial truth but the whole in context truth like Jesus did). Secondly, to not give in to temporary rewards that will give you long term pain and consequences. Thirdly, tell Satan to hit the road like Jesus did, "away from me, Satan." If you do these three things: see the temptation clearly, do not give in to temporary rewards, and tell Satan to leave, you will be able to "resist the devil" and watch him "flee from you." (James 4:7) We are tempted "when by (our) own evil desire, we are dragged away and enticed. Then, after desire has conceived, it gives birth to sin; and sin, when it is full-grown, gives birth to death" (James 1:14-15)

We all too often start the fire of temptation and if we don't put it out we will die in eternal fire! We do not need to be temptation arsonists who get so asphyxiated that we self-destruct in the smoke of temptation. Instead, if it smells like smoke, we need to leave it alone!

Lord, give us the wisdom You promise in James 1:5-8 so that we will not be "double-minded" or "prideful" and be overcome by the smoke of our own desires! Help us to know your Word, to remember Your truths, and to practice every day Your instruction. Amen.

- 11 -

If Unsettled Times Unsettle You

If unsettled times unsettle you, you may have a trust issue. By unsettled I'm not talking disturbed by the tragic losses of life from tsunamis, earthquakes, terrorists' exploits, or even material losses from Wall Street failures, bank collapses, or housing markets in the dumpster, etc. I am talking about sleeplessness, worry, high anxiety, that almost renders you non-functioning. The causes of unsettling times are as many as the grains of sand on a beach. From growing up in the USA from 1945 through 1970 let me recap a few events that truly unsettled us. Here is a partial list:

- The atom bomb developed and dropped on Hiroshima and Nagasaki to bring an end to WWII.

- The North Korea vs. South Korea conflict with our soldiers helping South Korea. All these years later and the USA military is still there.

- Sputnik put into orbit in October 1957 by the Soviet Union (USSR/ Russia) that catapulted the USA into the space race and the cold war. Along with Nikita Khrushchev's book, *I Will Bury You.*

- Civil unrest of the 1960's with race riots, marches, cities being burned, etc. (What happened to "love your neighbor" in the USA?)

- Assassinations: President John F. Kennedy, Dr. Martin Luther King, and Sen. Robert Kennedy. (What was going on within the USA?)

- Vietnam, anti-war protests, students being killed for protesting at places like Kent State. Vietnam veterans coming home to open public criticism, even being spit upon.

- President Regan's attempted assassination. He lived to lead and see the tearing down of the Berlin Wall in Germany. The great symbol of communism in our world crumbling as the west and the east residents of Berlin, Germany can become re-united in theory.

- Astronauts die before a world television audience as the Challenger spacecraft comes apart in an explosive fire. The USA and the world watched in disbelief.

- Another fiery scene holds our attention as the Branch Dividian compound is surrounded by FBI and ATF agents, then tanks and explosions, fire, and death of innocent people penetrate our minds. (Why?)

- A few years later and once again explosions and fire, panic, screams, and pain rip through us in the heartland as the Oklahoma City bombing stops life in the USA for a moment. (Why?)

- We will never forget September 11, 2001 as terrorists turn commercial airplanes into weapons wrecking families forever. From the fall of the Twin Towers to the Pentagon, to a field in Pennsylvania, the stories that unsettled us or even showed us American bravery began to pour forth out of that terrible day. This would lead us to unite for a short period and even truly seek God for awhile. It would also lead us into fears over color-coded issues about terror and our safety. It didn't stop there as we headed to war in Iraq, toppling Saddam Hussein, and to war in Afghanistan to keep the "al-Qaeda" terrorist network on the run. We would eventually get Osama Bin Laden, the master-mind of terror for "al-Qaeda."

- Earthquakes—major earthquakes from Haiti, to Chile, to Indonesia, to Japan have us quaking over possible devastating effects that continue to impact the world....with tsunamis, hurricanes, etc. Depending on damages to nuclear power plants, food sources, even oil spills we have many real concerns that can keep us unsettled.

In most of these listed they existed or exist in your macrocosm. They are very unsettling even if you are not a "big" picture, "world-view" kind of person. But let's come a little closer when looking at things that unsettle us. What do we do when someone very close to us....family member, friend, work associate dies? What happens when divorce is a reality, bringing pain and loss for everyone involved and even to some in your extended microcosm? Would losing your job, your home, or all your assets shake your stableness? Where would you go for help, or for some security?

Life has its bountiful repertoire of unsettling situations to shock you. Their sting will not leave you unaffected. Emotions are a real part of all of us. They can erupt when we are shocked with the tsunami that has hit our world. It happens again and again as I just illustrated in the 12 historical events mentioned, as well as the personal questions that I asked. There were many more significant unsettling events that I have not mentioned but witnessed as a public school administrator. Things like Title IX, Latch Key, cocaine, LSD, heroin, marijuana, gangs, meth, etc. also unsettled my world.

So what do we do? How can we possibly come thru these unsettling storms we face? Who can we turn to for help? Is there ever calm after a storm? Will it remain or last at least for a period of time? Does anyone ever get beyond being "unnerved" over "unsettling" events?

Allow me to begin to answer some of the questions with "Bible speak."

> May the Lord answer you when you are in distress; may the name of the God of Jacob protect you. May He send you help from the sanctuary and grant you support from Zion.
> — Psalm 20:1-2

> Some trust in chariots and some in horses, but we trust in the name of the Lord our God. They are brought to their knees and fall, but we rise up and stand firm.
> — Psalm 20:7-8

King David knew "on-going" unsettling events throughout his life. He learned that in all his times of emotional unsettledness there was One constant, The LORD ALMIGHTY. He "is the same yesterday, and today and forever." (Hebrews 13:8) No matter what it is that is unsettling to you, you can choose the Great Stabilizer, the Incomparable Guide, the Faithful Comforter, the Great Provider, the Ambassador of Hope, the Grantor of Prayers, yes, the Author of Peace in the midst of the storm—your storm.

Solomon said in Ecclesiastes 7:14, "When times are good, be happy; but when times are bad, consider: God has made one as well as the other. Therefore, a man cannot discover anything about his future." A little later in verse 18b Solomon tells us: "the man who fears God will avoid all extremes." No matter how unsettling life's *ifs* are, you can overcome with Christ by not getting caught up in the extreme "what ifs." "No one can comprehend what goes on under the sun. Despite all his efforts to search it out, man cannot discover its meaning. Even if a wise man claims he knows, he cannot really comprehend it." (Ecclesiastes 8:17b-d) Then Solomon says, "Anyone who is among the living has hope...." (Ecclesiastes 9:4a) Solomon concludes his search to finding the meaningfulness in life with all of its unsettling times with this instruction:

> Fear God and keep His commandments, For this is the whole duty of man. For God will bring everything into judgment, Including every hidden thing, Whether it is good or evil.
> — Ecclesiastes 12:13-14

We will face unsettling times in life. Jesus said it this way in Matthew 5:45b, "God causes his sun to rise on the evil and the good, and sends rain on the righteous and the unrighteous." The Apostle Paul also said,

> For it has been granted to you on behalf of Christ not only to believe on Him, but also to suffer for Him.
> — Philippians 1:29

Peter joins in with,

> If you are insulted because of the name of Christ, you are blessed, for the Spirit of glory and of God rests on you. If you suffer it should not be as a murderer or thief or any other kind of a criminal, or even as a meddler. However, if you suffer as a Christian, do not be ashamed, but praise God that you bear that name.
> — 1 Peter 4:14-16

We sometimes forget others are watching us, monitoring our behavior when we have become unsettled in unsettling times. Only with God, His Spirit residing in us, with His Truth filling our minds and hearts do we emerge as His servants with any impact on others when we been unsettled!

Unlike Solomon's key term "meaningless," the good news is we can find meaning for our unsettled times. Good can and does prevail over evil when you are totally surrendered to Jesus! Read the Bible, Jesus won over sin, the cross, the tomb, and Satan. He is in heaven, sitting at the Father's right hand (Mark 16:19b), cheering us on, praying for us to ask for help from Him. He won! He wants us to win (to be his witnesses—to have a vital, daily relationship with Him no matter what is going on). We can have His peace in the storms of life's unsettledness. We can be overcomers. He offers us everything we need to "keep on keeping on," as my old friend Jack Deverse used to say. Or as my good friend Reverend James Cullumber would say, "He props us up on every leaning side." Only a vital relationship with Christ can get us to those realizations!

When we realize the enemy's main tool in unsettledness is fear, we have a choice to make. Are we going to place our trust in a holy God who is all-powerful; who sent His only Son, Jesus, to save us; who fulfilled Jesus' promise that we would have The Comforter when He ascended to Heaven? Will we listen to any of His Scriptures that tell us "to fear not, for I am with you" (Isaiah 41:10) or allow Him to give us "a firm place to stand" (Psalm 40:2) while "He makes his (our) steps firm" (Psalm 37:23)? Maybe we need to hear what He told Joshua when his life became unsettled with Moses' death.

> I will be with you; I will never leave you nor forsake
> you. Be strong and courageous....Be strong and very
> courageous.
> — Joshua 1:5b *6a*

To be "strong and courageous" choose to trust God, regardless of what is unsettling you. He is trustworthy. Be encouraged in Christ and His truths no matter what it is that may have you unsettled.

Besides the twelve major unsettling events that I mentioned earlier, undoubtedly like most of you, I have let small things get to me. Yes, "the little foxes can spoil the vine." Little things can wear you down and cause you to be unsettled. Unlike some who preach "do not bother God with the small stuff. He gave you a brain. Use it," may I just testify to you that God has taught me to trust Him with the "small stuff." He cares about us, whether we are struggling with the "minute matters" or concerned over the "biggest of issues." He makes it very clear,

> Cast all your anxiety on him because he cares for you.
> — 1 Peter 5:7

> For the word of the Lord is right and true; He is faithful
> in all He does.
> — Psalm 33:4

Yes, "... the Lord's unfailing love surrounds the man who trusts in Him" (Psalm 32:10b & 10c)

> See, I lay in Zion a stone that causes men to stumble and
> a rock that makes them fall, and the one (that could be
> you) who trusts in Him will never be put to shame.
> — Romans 9:33

May we overcome the fear or fears that unsettle us, by putting our trust in Jesus Christ, our Lord and Savior!

- 12 -

If You Feel Abandoned,
Alone, and Trapped

The *if* in life hits like an "EF-5" Oklahoma twister when you feel abandoned, alone and trapped. Add to that list "forgotten" and the aftermath of your personal feelings bring a sense of doom and despair. There seems to be no bright days forecast for your future, just the gloom of generated feelings that say; you are alone, you have been abandoned, you have been forgotten, and there is the sense of no way out—trapped! Yes, the enemy of your soul and mine loves to get those feelings swirling, twisting in our mind. If not brought into check by God's truths, each day can be filled with doom.

God's chosen people, collectively and individually, have had these experiences from time to time. For example, the children of Israel (as told by Moses in Deuteronomy 4) are being warned not to break the covenant God is making with them. He is also telling them if they do, what will happen. Enter some of the feelings of this chapter into Israel's thinking. Listen to what God promises.

> But if from there you seek the Lord your God, you will find Him if you look for Him with all your heart and with all your soul. When you are in distress and all these things have happened to you, then in later days you will return to the Lord your God and obey Him. For the Lord your God is a merciful God; He will not abandon or destroy you or forget the covenant....
>
> — Deuteronomy 4:29-31

What was true for Israel is true today for God's people. There is One who knows exactly where you are. Do not buy into the feelings of abandonment or aloneness. If you have given your heart to Jesus, you are never alone!

We are all subject to these times where feelings of abandonment, aloneness, being forgotten or trapped raise havoc with how we face life. I've been fortunate to have had some great Christian examples and mentors. I've also been blessed to know some very well-known leaders from different professions as well as from his Bride. From their lips would come statements—actual accounts of treatment—after years of distinguished, selfless serving that spoke about their feelings of being forgotten, alone, abandoned, even trapped.

One leader who served as one of the international generals of a denomination for many years stated: "The church brought me to the Hoosier Dome in a limo to preside at my last official general assembly. When it was over, I literally had to call my own cab to get home." This is a true story that has always spoken to me about how thoughtless we can be for people who are supposed to be very caring and compassionate. When I called another retired district superintendent about preaching revival services at the church I was pastoring, he stated, "Bob, I would love to come. Yours is the first phone call from anyone in the church I have had in over 2 years. I've felt alone and forgotten." This was hard to believe because this great man of God was previously in high demand as a Spirit-filled, effective communicator. There was always good fruit from his ministry. But his voice over the phone told me how much he was struggling with his alone, abandoned, forgotten feelings. What if that was normal reality? My time would come when facing those feelings would need to be addressed. So here we are, addressing the reality that we will all face. The reality of how to handle the feelings of aloneness, abandonment, being forgotten or trapped.

First of all we must reach the place where we know that we know we are not alone. If we have God's spirit, who is available to us, we will know we are not alone. Yet in our humanness we may allow loneliness or lack of human interactions to dictate the thought that we are alone, even when we know differently deep within our mind. Just look at the prophet Elijah in 1 Kings 18. He has already talked with Obadiah, a devout believer in the Lord. He is now on Mount Carmel facing one of the toughest tests of his prophetic life, being outnumbered 450 to 1 (talk about stress). Elijah throws out the challenge to the prophets of Baal.

> Then Elijah addresses the people of Israel with "how long will you waver between two opinions? If the Lord is God, follow Him; but if Baal is God follow him!" But the people said nothing. Then Elijah said to them, "I am the only one of the Lord's prophets left,...."
> — 1 Kings 18:21-22

Wait a minute Elijah, you must be having spiritual dementia, what about Obadiah? The showdown takes place. God answers Elijah's prayer with a supernatural fire show for the people to witness. Then King Ahab tells Queen Jezebel that her Baal prophets have been slaughtered by Elijah. Jezebel makes her threats to kill Elijah known to him. Now we witness this Mount Carmel melt-down as Elijah runs for his life! Elijah runs for a whole day into the desert. Aloneness has set in as Elijah voices his fears by "I have had enough, Lord, take my life…" (1 Kings 19:4)

After some more personal drama from Elijah's fears we hear the Lord's words to Elijah. "What are you doing here, Elijah?" (1 Kings 19:9b)

Now hear the pitiful cry of Elijah who feels abandoned, alone, and yes, trapped by Jezebel's threat. "I am the only one left, and now they are trying to kill me too." (1Kings 19:10c) The Lord gives Elijah instructions as He gets his attention.

Then the Lord says to Elijah "go back the way you came" (1Kings 19:15) …..and He tells Elijah: "I reserve seven thousand in Israel—all whose knees have not bowed down to Baal and all whose mouths have not kissed him." (1 Kings 19:18)

Undeniably anyone, even the greatest of God's servants—even God's only son, can have times when feelings of aloneness, abandonment, and being trapped can manifest themselves. It is up to each person when feelings deceive and the reality of God and His truths are hidden to "go back to the way you came." In other words go back to (remember) the times when God passed by and spoke to you through a Bible promise or a Christian friend or a phrase in a Christian song. During those times you knew God's Spirit was with you and you were not alone. You chose to believe. You trusted God! He does not abandon His children. You need to believe God's Word again. Treat your doubts like you should handle a telemarketer: Don't pick up the phone! May I tell you, hold securely to your faith regardless of how you are feeling? I get regular calls from a very elderly parishioner of one of my former pastorates. As I tell you her story, you will see a *what if* terrifying, yet too often repeated, collision with feeling alone, abandoned, and trapped at this time in her life.

For several decades this lady and her deceased husband walked with God, gave to others unselfishly, and served in their local church. When her husband died a couple years ago she sold her home in the USA and headed to live with her youngest son in the Philippines. She left her life savings, her monthly retirement stipends in her bank accounts in the U.S.A. They were to be overseen by her oldest stepson who was to send her money as she requested it. In a matter of a very short time she faced the following: her youngest son became very ill and wheelchair bound at best, no familiar church or friends or family except for her very ill son, a stepson who refuses to send her her money, a country she is totally unfamiliar with, and her last living sibling's death. When she calls, I hear "Where is God?" "Does He still love me?" "Is He here with me?" "Have I been abandoned?" "My stepson won't even send me the money so I can come home, but I don't have a home anymore." "I couldn't even get the money to come home for my sister's funeral." "I'm so alone."

As a minister for over thirty-five years, I wish I could tell you that this is the only account I've known about like this. Unfortunately, I've known of too many family members who ripped off other family members, especially those in the over sixty age bracket.

What would you tell the lady who now resides penniless, trapped with her wheelchair-bound son in the Philippines?

How do you understand a situation like I've just described? She has definitely had a *what if* collision with life. Dealing with feelings takes courage. It takes a conscious choice to say I will believe. I will trust God. I will put my faith in Him and His Word no matter how I feel. The great thing about faith is that you do not have to understand to believe. A child doesn't understand nutrition but chooses to eat what his/her mother feeds him/her—that is faith! Abraham had no clue about where God was taking him but chose to go, obeying God. The Bible says,

> By faith Abraham…obeyed and went, even though he did not know where he was going.
>   — Hebrews 11:8

Read chapter 11 of Hebrews to get a picture of heroes of faith. Faith has nothing to do with understanding! For this lady I just told you about, even though she has been grievously wronged, experienced great loss, it will be her choice of faith that will get her to Heaven. Her faith will not leave her abandoned. Her faith will break the trapped barriers. God will not leave her nor will He leave you, if you belong to Him! Yes, He gives us the gift of time and the freedom to choose as long as we live on planet earth. Where are you placing your faith today?

Do you know that feelings are often deceptive and very draining? When you are a victim to feelings it is like running on a treadmill. You expend energy but you are going nowhere! You will be trapped on that emotional treadmill unless you consciously choose to have faith in God. Trusting God to be bigger, and more powerful than your circumstances and feelings, you believe in Him. The greatest hurdle to choosing faith will not be your circumstances, it will be self. God wants us to believe, to be bold with our prayer requests. Sometimes in football games the time will be almost gone. The trailing team's quarterback has one more desperate opportunity to pull out a victory. So the quarterback rolls out or drops back and throws a "hail Mary" pass hoping his receiver will catch it for the game winning touchdown. Maybe that describes what you need to do today, throw a "hail Mary" prayer, trusting the Receiver to catch it? If you have had or are having feelings of being alone, abandoned, or trapped, throw God a prayer of faith! God is not intimidated by big requests or bothered with small requests. He is insulted when we do not ask and believe! As Jesus told the synagogue ruler, Jarius, regarding his daughter, "don't be afraid; just believe." (Mark 5:36b)

> .....run with perseverance the race marked out for us. Let us fix our eyes on Jesus, the Author and Perfector of our faith....
>
> — Hebrews 12:1

God will make a way for you when you trust Him. You do not have to live feeling abandoned, alone or trapped!

- 13 -

Why Do *What Ifs* Eat At Us?

The worrisome *what ifs* can potentially rob you of living life! To lose your ability to live life to the full because of *what ifs* is a travesty of the worst kind. When our *what ifs* propel us to go through the motions of living, to basically be an imitation of a person living, we need to understand what is behind our *what ifs*. So what is really behind many of our *what ifs*? Pure and simple behind most of our *what ifs* is a 4 letter word, FEAR! You see fear at work at a very early age. Make a loud noise and watch a baby's reaction. The baby may jump just because of being shocked by the noise. The baby may scream. The baby may cry because of his or her fear of the loud noise. Fear has done its number on the baby as it translates the loud noise into *what if*. Unfortunately as adults it is fear that is really behind the majority of our *what ifs*. Fear is anxious anticipation of ____ (you fill in your fear). Fear is an anxiety or concern. Fear is all too often irrational, our thinking has become flawed and we place our faith in the wrong things.

Facing our *what ifs* matters because then we can identify our fear or fears and begin to give them to God. Once again we are looking deeply into our *what ifs*. When we do, we can identify the fear or fears which reveals where we trust God the least. Ouch! If fear is placing faith or focusing our mental, emotional, spiritual, and even physical energy on the wrong thing, we need to address the deep issue of trust.

Besides loud noises, babies are afraid of falling. These two fears, loud noises and falling, have been proven by researchers to be a baby's biggest fears. So beyond the fear of falling for a baby—learning how to stand, and eventually walk, is the issue of trust. Will a piece of furniture stay permanent so that the baby can trust it for support? Will a parent really hold on and not let me fall? Trust is the key behind our fears that are cleverly camouflaged in our *what ifs*. There is a popular song chorus that has the phraseology "if our God is for us, who could ever stop us." We need that kind of mentality, that kind of trust in God, as we face the *what ifs* (fears) in life. David got to that place when he said,

> I sought the Lord, and He answered me: He delivered me from all my fears.
> — Psalm 34:4

Are you trusting God with all of your life? Are you trusting God with what you value the most? Faith in God or placing your trust in God is the key to dealing with life's *what ifs*. John Wesley said,

> Whenever I feel fearful emotions overtaking me I just close my eyes and thank God that He is still on the throne reigning over everything and I take comfort in His control over all the affairs my life.

Is there an area of your life where you are not trusting God? Does it cost you sleep? The Bible tells us "God will keep in perfect peace him whose mind is steadfast, because he trusts in God." (Isaiah 26:3)

Could it be as simple as a trust issue that *what ifs* eat away at our total being? President Theodore Roosevelt said, "If you could kick the person in the pants responsible for most of your trouble, you wouldn't sit for a month." Yes, we are our own worst enemy! We beat ourselves to death with *what ifs* when we do not recognize *what ifs* as fear, and choose to overcome our fear by trusting a Holy, sovereign God. We need to trust His promises to us, His children. We have the freedom to choose where we put our trust and in whom. If we would stop spending most of our time thinking about the temporary and choose to spend more time thinking about the eternal, it would help us to consciously trust God.

> Don't live any longer the way this world lives. Let your thinking be completely changed. Then, you will be able to test what God wants for you. And you will agree that what He wants is right....
> — Romans 12:2 NIV

He is saying, renew your thinking. The Message says it this way,

> Don't become so well-adjusted to your culture that you fit into it without even thinking. Instead, fix your attention on God. You'll be changed from the inside out....
> — Romans 12:2 MSG

When you think outside of culture or the temporary, you will think differently. The fears or *what ifs* regarding your time, your money, and your relationships will be different. You will not give in to your *what ifs*, when you live a life of trust in God. "Therefore I tell you, whatever you ask for in prayer, believe that you received it, and it will be yours." (Mark 11:24) Living out your trust matters because you will pray and see answers..."the prayer of a righteous man is powerful and effective." (James 5:16) God listens to the one who does His will. (See John 9:31) With God, with His promises and your trust in Him, you will live without nagging fear! "God's divine power has given us everything we need for life......" (2 Peter 1:3)

Let God remake you to be fearless! Let God remake you to be courageous! Listen! You will hear from God. "My sheep listen to my voice; I know them, and they follow Me." (John 10:27) Will you follow Him out of the valley of fear into the land of trust? If you do, you will enter into a new era in your life where choosing to trust will be your first response instead of letting fear devour you! You will have a peace because you have chosen to trust God.

> You will keep in perfect peace him whose mind is steadfast, because he trusts you.
> — Isaiah 26:3

Can you see yourself steadfast, and peaceful? Trust the Lord and find His peace that will quell your *what ifs*.

- 14 -

What *If* a Negative Title Has Been Attached to Your Name?

If a negative label has been attached to your name, good news....with God that can be changed. God specializes in breaking negative titles or stereotyped images that bind us. How you ask? He has ways, but once again it starts with our choices and relationship with Him. God specializes (I know I've already said this but I really want you to take hold of this) in breaking the negative labels! He is the Creator God who can change things and make them new. We can change with God and become His new creation.

Biblically, let us look at some examples of people who carried a negative title until they had an encounter with God and responded to Him in true repentance and obedience. Watch what happens!

Adulteress, slut, tramp were all titles the townspeople attached to her. She would hear the whispers of these titles. They could be heard whenever she ventured out in public. She probably had chosen to ignore them, to pretend they weren't real. Yet she had her moments when the truth about her reputation would put her face to face with her negative titles. But today she just wanted to get water from Jacob's well. It should be uneventful. Just simply go to the well, fill the water jar, and get back home. Hopefully, no encounters with knowledgeable people who would be happy to mention a negative title or two to her.

Upon arriving at the well where she was going to draw water, she encountered Jesus. He asks her for a drink of water. Her response because of cultural backgrounds is, "how can you (a Jew) ask me (a Samaritan woman) for a drink?

Jesus responds with, "if you knew the gift of God and who it is that asks you for a drink, you would have asked him and he would have given you living water." (John 4:7-10) Living water? She questions, "Where can I get this living water?" Jesus tells her,

> Everyone who drink this water will be thirsty again, but whoever drinks the water I give...will never thirst again...it will become in him (or her) a spring of water welling up to eternal life.
>
> — John 4:11-14

I think it is noteworthy that Jesus told her if she asked she would receive living water (forgiveness and life eternal). He lays the groundwork for a new life, unwanted titles changed. Yes, He does this before He lets her know He knows all about her past five husbands and how the man she's living with now is not her husband. In this case, her sins had brought her the negative titles. Look what Jesus does after letting her know He knows. He gives her hope by letting her know she has met the Messiah and Jesus tells her how to have life regardless of past negative titles!

Sometimes a negative title will call for a disconnect, an alias, yes, even a name change. But more importantly, it will start with a heart change. It will come with clarity that will call for a conscious decision. It happened that way for Saul on a purposeful trip to Damascus where he intended to take Christ-followers captive. With zeal he earned the title of feared bounty-hunter. With zeal he would "breathe out murderous threats against the Lord's disciples" whether man or woman. Remember it was Saul who watched and condoned Stephen's death. (That mental picture of Stephen's testimony before dying haunted this accomplice to murder.)

Watch what happens as Saul, the bounty-hunter, persecutor, and accomplice to murder nears Damascus.

> ...suddenly a light from heaven flashed around him. He fell to the ground and heard a voice say to him, Saul, Saul, why do you persecute me?" "Who are you, Lord?" Saul asked. (Isn't it amazing Saul knew to call him Lord?) "I am Jesus whom you are persecuting," He replied. "Now get up and go to the city, and you will be told what you must do." (Saul's first test after encountering Jesus? To be obedient and follow instruction.) The men traveling with Saul stood there speechless; they heard the sound but did not see anyone. Saul got up from the ground, but when he opened his eyes he could see nothing. So they led him by the hand into Damascus. For three days he was blind and did not eat or drink anything. (Hardly the picture of the most feared persecutor on his mission to take Christ-followers prisoner.)
>
> — Acts 9:1-9

You can read Acts for the details of Saul who became the great Gentile missionary, gospel writer with his letters (books in the Bible). Saul said yes to Jesus, was converted and got a new name, Paul. In time it would be this new alias that people would remember as a devout, zealous, wholly devoted follower of Jesus Christ.

If the adulterous woman at the well could be changed and a Christ persecutor like Saul could be changed to be an admired Christ-follower named Paul, why not you or me?

There are definitely many more Biblical examples, from crooked tax-collectors like Zacchaeus to the woman caught in the act of adultery and brought to Jesus by those who wanted to trap Jesus. (See John 8:1-11) There are so many who would attest to the fact...Jesus can change the negative title or image that is attached to your name.

Allow me to share a true story about a professional athlete that I had the privilege of sharing Christ with who asked Jesus into his heart. His is a powerful story that, with God's help, I will put into words for the sake of helping anyone who reads them.

This world-champion was known as the "baby-faced assassin." Most recently he was known for his drug use which cost him his "World-Champion" title. With champion belts gone, he turned to drugs. On a high he threatened to kill his wife, who called for help. When the police arrived they found him strung-out with a loaded handgun and a very, very scared loving wife. It was his wife who, while at the hair dresser's, got my name and came to see me at my pastor's office. As she told me her story and her fears, she also told me she was hiding at a girl friend's house because her husband had gotten out of jail on bond. That day she asked Jesus into her heart! We asked God for her protection and wisdom to know what to say and what to do with her husband. Eventually after many talks, she moved back in. Being changed by Jesus, she began to show her ex-world champion the love from the One true World-Champion. This led to him asking her what happened to her to be able to forgive him. She told him, and he sought me out.

His words to my receptionist and also to my secretary were, "where is the man who messed with my wife?" Both ladies were scared because they had seen his face on the national news and knew he was waiting to stand trial for his threats to his wife and his drug use.

"Pastor, the baby-faced assassin is here and he wants to talk with you NOW."

As I opened my door, there stood an agitated 116 pound world champion fighter who definitely wanted to see me. I said come into my office... good to meet you or something to that effect, all the while praying "God, you knew all about this moment, please help me to know what to say and what to do."

"Man," he said, "what did you do to my wife?"

I responded with, "What do you mean?"

"She is not the same. She has forgiven me for holding a loaded pistol to her head and telling her I was going to blow her brains out. What did you do to her?"

"I simply told her about Jesus, God's Son, the Savior, who could change her heart and life and protect her if she'd ask forgiveness for her sins and ask Jesus to come into her heart, to allow Him to be in control. Your wife did that and we prayed for her and for you!"

He looked puzzled. He started talking about what she was doing (which was acts of forgiveness) and that she told him again and again she forgave him and wanted to move back home! (WOW, was my thought, even though I had witnessed many miracles of changed lives it is still amazing what God can do when people obey Him.)

Then I remember silently praying, "Lord, you want to assassinate this baby-faced assassin, help me to talk his street language which I don't know or give me some way to get through to him so he will understand what you did." In shock, I heard myself saying, "Listen up. God isn't going to spar any longer with you. He is through with your shadow boxing (making excuses). Today you have to make a decision. This is it. Show time. Show up or leave!" (I still can't believe that I verbalized those words.) But this champion who couldn't stand still, who had been moving around talking to me (like dancing in the ring before a fight) stopped in his tracks.

He looked at me and said, "Man, preacher man, I want what she got!"

I had witnessed God's Holy Spirit KO the baby-faced assassin. I explained the salvation message, called two associate ministers from their offices, and headed for the altar with my stunned world-champ. At the altar I explained to him what he was about to do. I asked him if he understood and wanted Christ in his heart. A tear-stained cheek and fighter's determined stare faced me and with an emphatic "yes" that filled the almost empty sanctuary. That day at that altar with three ministers praying for the champ, Christ entered his heart and started a new work.

The road ahead was going to be tough, even long at times but the champ, with his wife and his new "preacher-man," were going to witness miracles. Let me continue to tell you two more parts of this true story that are truly miracles.

The 3 time champ was a broken, fearful, anxious pugilist who had never known defeat in the "squared-circle," but now defeat was eminent as he awaited his trial date. He had chosen to have a judge rule on the verdict rather than a jury. The charge "assault with a deadly weapon" loomed before him as he counted down the days to his trial. The 9 AM time and date finally arrived. As promised, I met the champ and his wife in the hallway outside the courtroom at 8:30 AM. We listened to the champ, who poured out his fears about being sent to prison, etc. His wife took his hands and put them on her cheeks. Their eyes fixed on each other. These two new believers were in for a long day, but she said, "With Jesus it is okay."

"Pastor, it will be okay, right?"

I took both their hands and said, "One thing I know, God's kids can trust God. He will help today. You'll be able to face the *ifs* today because of Jesus."

Little did I know as we sat together in the courtroom that the judge kept pushing back the champ's time for other cases. I noticed at different times throughout the day the judge kept looking back at the champ, his wife, and me. (I believe it was his strategy to watch their behavior, plus wear down the circus of reporters who had filled the courtroom.)

Finally at 4 PM the court clerk called for the champ and his attorney to come forward.

The champ turned to me and said, What am I going to do? I can't go to prison. I'll never survive being locked up in a cell."

I said, "Champ, just tell the truth. Jesus will help you."

The judge stared at the champ. The charges of assault were read as it described him holding the loaded revolver to his wife's head and threatening to kill her.

The judge said, "How do you plead, guilty or not guilty?" Silence filled the courtroom. Reporters edged up to the front of their seats. Silence. Once again the judge said, "Guilty or not guilty?"

The champ finally broke his silence and said, "Guilty, your honor." Gasps now broke the silence as the reporters and spectators were expecting a long trial, and a battle to get the champ off.

The judge was visually taken back as he rocked backwards in his chair and just stared at the champ. He then looked back at the champ's wife and asked, "Who are you, young lady?"

She answered, "His wife."

"And the man seated next to you?"

"He is our new pastor."

The judge asked the champ's wife to come forward. She did. As she stood before the judge, he asked her why she was here today sitting next to the champ.

She told the judge, "He is my husband and I have forgiven him. It was the drugs that night, not him."

"Are you back with him, living as husband and wife?"

"Yes, your honor."

"Aren't you afraid?"

"No, your honor."

"Why?"

"Your honor we have both asked Jesus into our hearts. Life is different now."

The judge paused and then said, "You may return to your seat." He then turned his questions toward the champ. "Do you realize how fortunate you are to not only have a wife that loves you, but who has forgiven you?"

The champ replied, "Yes, your honor."

I could see the two prosecuting attorneys fidgeting in their seats. They were not pleased with the champ's guilty plea. I'm sure they were looking forward to lots of TV time and press coverage. That was gone. Today was going to be it. The judge said there would be a 30 minute recess and then he would issue the sentence for the champ's punishment. Thirty minutes seemed like thirty years for the champ, his wife, and myself.

The judge returned and the champ and his attorney stood awaiting the judge's decision. The judge said, "I am sentencing you to three years' probation with the understanding that if you violate any terms of the probation you will go to prison for the maximum number of years for this crime. You have been given another chance; don't blow it. You can thank your wife and the fact that you were truthful with me. You were the only defendant I heard truth from all day."

The prosecutors loudly voiced their objections until the judge's gavel came down with a "bang" and the judge's voice saying, "So ruled." Then he walked down to the champ and his wife, looked at them both, nodded and said, "I hope you have a long and happy life together."

God had ruled that day by working an unheard of miracle through a very hard, strict-sentencing judge!

As the weeks passed God was very much at work in the hearts of the champ and his wife. He had gone to a drug rehab center. He had gotten free from cocaine, his drug of choice. He had been re-instated to box again and after a few fights, would soon get to fight and win back his world champion title. Life had certainly changed for the better for this "young-in-Christ" couple.

Let's fast forward several months. My wife and I were tucked away in the Big Cimarron country of the Colorado Rockies for a week of much needed rest. The retreat-secluded cabin was a welcome relief from the demands of a rapidly growing church in the largest New Mexican city. On Friday I received an urgent message that conveyed I needed to call the world-champion's wife immediately. For a few seconds my mind raced to the worst, negative *what if* possibilities. I prayed and made the call. When she answered, I immediately said, "Are you okay? What about the champ? Is he okay?"

"Yes, I am okay! But we have a very serious problem."

"What is it?" I asked.

"It is the champ. He has this nationally televised championship fight tomorrow at the Duke's stadium. But he doesn't want to fight anymore. He says, he won't fight until he has talked with you. Pastor, we are under contract. The TV media is here. The fight is sold out. It has been promoted for months. Where are you? Can you come to him now?"

I proceeded to explain that I was over 12 hours' away and wasn't scheduled to come back until next week. Then I heard myself saying, "I guess if we went back to the cabin, packed, and drove through the night we could probably be there by 1:30" (a half hour before the fight was to begin). She told me to come to a certain gate and she would have ring-side seats waiting for my wife and me. Maybe she thought the champ would fight if he knew I would be there.

As we drove through the night and arrived at the stadium about 25 minutes before fight time, I prayed for God's Spirit to grant wisdom to know what to say to the champ. I knew his story well as he had shared with me how he got the title "baby-faced" assassin. Let me share that in synoptic form before I conclude this story and this chapter.

When our champ was just a young boy his mother was taken by several men, raped several times, and stabbed multiple times until she died. The champ never really knew his absentee father. He was left with grandparents in a small dirt floored house and the city streets to grow up. He lived on food out of alley dumpsters while growing up. He got involved in boxing at a local gym (boy's club) while growing up. He learned the pugilistic skills very well. He had extremely quick hands that broke opponent's noses, jaws, ribs, as well as inflicting major cuts to faces. He was a fierce fighter who tried to hurt his opponents because, as he told me, "each time I step into the squared-circle I imagine my opponent as one of my mother's killers." It is no wonder that this baby-faced champion was undefeated, knocking out a majority of his opponents. He was fighting his mother's killers with a purpose to inflict great bodily harm.

Which brings us back to the stadium with a champion who didn't want to fight. As we entered the gate and were ushered to our ring-side seats, the champ's wife came to us. She thanked us for coming to the stadium and asked if I would follow her to the champ's dressing room.

"Pastor," she said, "he says he will not fight. I hope you can talk to him. We have a contract, and you see all the people here, as well as the TV networks, Sugar Ray Leonard and Dan Dierdorf. They are in the locker room with him. I hope you can talk to him."

As we entered the packed locker room I couldn't even see the champ. But his wife motioned to his bodyguard, and told him to get me to the champ. The noise in the locker room was deafening. After pushing past some of the celebrities, I could see the champ seated over in the corner by himself, head down in his taped-up hands.

"Champ, can we talk?" I said. He looked up, got up, and hugged me.

"Pastor, I need to talk to you. I do not want to fight anymore. I can't look at my opponents as my mother's killers any more. I see them differently now and do not want to hurt them. I just don't think I can ever step in the ring again. Now I'm here to fight and defend the championship in my hometown and I can't do it. What will I do? Will you pray for me?"

"Of course, champ, we'll pray. I'm going to pray that God will lead you in whether or not you fight today, or ever again. I'm going to ask Him to help you to know what to do, and to know with Him 'all things are possible.' It hasn't been that many months ago since you watched God work a miracle in the courtroom. If He did that for you then, He can help you today!"

"You're right, pastor. There is so much noise in here. I like it quiet when I pray."

"The champ wants to pray, so please bow your heads, I found myself yelling."

The locker room full of reporters, and celebrities, became silent. I can't remember all of my prayer but God's Spirit was there.

When I said "AMEN," I looked at the champ and he was aglow. His face had a smile on it, and he said, "I know I have to fight this fight today and then we'll go from here one step at a time."

As I watched him fight, I thought: another miracle—an unlikely one in an unlikely place where a "baby-faced" assassin's world was changed from the inside out in front of thousands of witnesses that day, not only in Duke stadium but all over TV land.

If God can change your author, an adulteress woman, a zealous Saul, and a three-time world champion, drug-using boxer, He can change your negative *if!*

- 15 -

If You Think Your Heart is Hard

If you think your heart is hard, you probably wouldn't be reading this, nor would you want to read it. One of the great lies that the enemy of our soul likes to perpetuate is that of having committed the unforgivable or unpardonable sin because of an uncaring, hardened heart. People sometimes reach this point thinking that there is no hope for them, and that their hard heart is too far gone. It is interesting what the Bible says by way of instruction as well as warning. Listen and think about some of these Scriptures.

> Today, if you hear His voice, do not harden your hearts as you did in the rebellion...
> — Romans 3:7b-8a

> See to it, brothers that none of you has a sinful, unbelieving heart that turns away from the living God.
> — Hebrews 3:12

> ...so that none of you may be hardened by sin's deceitfulness.
> — Hebrews 3:13b

And again the warning,

> ...if you hear His voice, do not harden your hearts as you did in the rebellion.
> — Hebrews 3:15

Biblically we are being instructed that we have a choice "...not to harden our hearts" and to follow through or to act.

> If we deliberately keep on sinning after we have received the knowledge of truth, no sacrifice for sins is left, but only fearful expectation of judgment....
> — Hebrews 10:26-27a

Those warnings do not nullify Christ's forgiveness and love, but they do speak to us about how we think and how we act. The choice is ours. "So do not throw away your confidence; it will be richly rewarded." (Hebrews 10:35) Paul also warned us about our choices...

> But because of your stubbornness and your unrepentant heart, you are storing up wrath against yourself for the day of God's wrath, when His righteous judgment will be revealed. God will give to each person according to what he has done.
> — Romans 2:5-6

Therefore, in context the message of Christ is "forgiveness and that He does not want anyone to perish." Forgiveness is available to anyone no matter what, if the person chooses not to harden his/her heart. Christ does not harden the heart. That is each person's choice! We need to listen to the Word and not be deceived by the enemy's words or our own self negative talk that penetrates our heart.

God's truth teaches us "we are His house, if we hold on to our courage and the hope of which we boast." (Hebrews 3:6)

> Today, if you hear His voice, do not harden your hearts....
> — Hebrews 3:7b-8a

We need to hear those words over and over again if we are struggling with thoughts about our heart being hardened.

> If my people, who are called by my name, will humble
> themselves and pray and seek my face and turn from their
> wicked ways, then I will hear from heaven and forgive
> their sin and will heal their land.
>
> — 2 Chronicles 7:14

God's Words of instruction are for a nation of "hardened-type" hearts, Israel. You talk about selfish and stubborn, just look at God's chosen people. You see God's *if* calls for us to make a choice to (1) humble ourselves, (2) to pray, (3) to seek His face, and (4) to turn from their (our) wicked ways (this is selfish, self-absorbed thinking that deceives). If we do what He said, healing will be ours. We can have sensitive, softened hearts because of Jesus being in charge.

You may be saying I don't know God like that. You can if you choose to. You can have a close, current relationship if you start to believe His promises and choose to act upon them.

As David told his son Solomon, "If you seek Him, He will be found by you" (1 Chronicles 28:9b).

Moses told the people of Israel ".....if from there (where you are) you seek the Lord your God, you will find Him if you look for Him with all your heart and with all your soul" (Deuteronomy 4:29).

Choice is the key to how we begin to face the *if* in life. From the beginning of civilization as we know it, God gave the first man and the first woman choice. They could enjoy all, eat from all the different trees in the garden except from one tree (See Genesis 3:8-17). They had it made. But God gave them choice just as He does for us. Adam and Eve blew it, threw it all away...the living forever/no dying, free food/no working for it, etc. Why? Because they gave in to being deceived in their minds and chose to eat from the only tree that was off limits. They did what self wanted to do. I wonder how self got so elevated that self could choose to ignore "off limits...do not eat." Oh, there was another voice in the garden planting doubt, wasn't there? A voice that said, "Did God really say, 'you must not eat from...'" (Genesis 3:1b). "You will not surely die..." (Genesis 3:4a)

Do not let voices or the enemy plant the *if* to cause you to doubt. Do not let him cause you to doubt that God loves you or to believe your heart is too hard for God. It is amazing with all the knowledge we possess that we will choose to throw away our relationship with God. It is worth repeating that Adam and Eve made their choice and paid the price just as God said. Mankind has had to deal with all the ramifications of their sinful choices. God did not want a robotic Adam or a robotic Eve. He wanted them to choose to love Him and to have a vital personal, daily relationship with Him.

He still wants that with you and me. That is why He sent Jesus Christ to die on the cross, paying the price for mankind's sins, so that we can have a personal relationship with God no matter what *if* in life we are facing or even struggling with in our heart.

> For God so loved the world (you & me) that He gave His one and only Son, that whoever believes in Him shall not perish but have eternal life. For God did not send His Son (Jesus) into the world to condemn the world, but to save the world (you & me) through Him.
> — John 3:16-17

In over 35 plus years of ministry I have met some hearts that were in a bad state because of *if* and the doubt involved. But with the hardest of hearts in this group, no one was too far gone for God's grace to soften. No heart was too hard for God. How you face the *if* in life is a choice. It is your choice. You do not have to face it alone. You can face the *if* in life every day. You may face your next *if* with Him. I may not have met you, but unequivocally I can say, your heart is not too hard for God.

- 16 -

If Childlike Faith Escapes You

At two years of age one of our daughters exhibited great faith in me and my ability to catch her no matter where she jumped from, be it a diving board, a rock, or the top of a ladder. It really helped me if I knew she was jumping. If childlike faith is anything we could define, it might be defined as unquestioning trust. When someone exhibits childlike faith, that unquestioning trust, he/she comes across as fearless. What if you could say, "I have no fear?" What would your world look like? How would it be changed?

You would have a deep peace that as the Bible says, "would be beyond comprehension." A peace that when it encounters *if,* translates to maybe or to hopefulness. A peace that releases a person from being a prisoner to *if, what if,* and *if only.* Childlike faith brings forth an unquenchable, energized determination. That determination with God and His promises brings possibilities instead of gloomy impossibilities. *If* becomes a stepping stone to see God work in and through you!

My daughter was a fearless daredevil as long as she knew dad was around to catch her. You can become a fearless daredevil of faith when you know that Dad (your heavenly Father) is there for you. Without that trust you cannot live the faith life. Without that trust *if* in its various forms becomes your C4 (plastic explosive) that detonates, leaving behind a wasted, doubt-ridden, fearful life. God's Word says just "mustard seed" sized faith (trust in God) will bring peace and hope.

Where do you start to be able to have the faith I have been sharing with you?

1. Start where you are.

2. Ask Jesus Christ to forgive you of any doubt or sin.

3. Ask Jesus to enter your heart and take control.

4. Let go of your doubts and fears.

5. Imagine God's hand reaching down to take hold of your hand no matter where you are or what you have done.

6. Be a faith daredevil. (Make the choice!)

7. Jump into your Heavenly Father's arms. (He will catch you. He is trustworthy.)

Jesus tells us "....He Himself is our peace.." (Ephesians 2:4a).

> Peace I leave with you; My Peace I give to you; not as the world gives do I give to you. Do not let your heart be troubled, nor let it be fearful.
> — John 14:27

He makes it very clear the choice is ours to have peace (no fear) or not to have peace. The provision is there. The price has been paid to eradicate any troubled heart if the individual chooses to act.

Transforming peace to overcome *if* does come from God. It is "...the peace of God, which surpasses all understanding which will guard your hearts

and minds in Christ Jesus" (Philippians 4:7). You know He is available!
Use your mustard seed of faith and be God's fearless daredevil. He will
not drop you!

- 17 -

Are You an Impact Player or
Are You an Impressionist?

Years ago when I was a head football and baseball coach, I watched for "impact players." For those who are unfamiliar with athletics let me give you a very brief education. Coaches definitely want impact players. These are the athletes who possess the ability to change the outcome of a game in a matter of a few seconds or minutes. Coaches learn quickly (or they are out of a job) the difference between an impact player, a player, and an impressionist. One can win you the game. One will keep you in the game. One will cost you the game. So my *what if* question is "what if you were an impact player, not merely a player, or an impressionist?" How would your everyday world change? What would you have to do to become an impact player?

- Are you an impact player? yes or no

- Are you a player? yes or no

- Are you an impressionist? yes or no

Before I explain how someone can become an impact player, let me define player and impressionist for the sake of understanding. A player is someone who is on the team, who contributes to a degree to the team, and wants the team to achieve its goal(s). A player may never stand out or on rare occasions have a stand out performance that gets limited press or attention. Does a player work hard? Most of the time. Does a player have unwavering faith in the team's ability to emerge victorious or successful? Most of the time. Can a player be counted upon to deliver what is needed, when it is needed? Most of the time. Does a player ever allow doubt to creep in and affect his/her performance? Once in a while.

The impressionist is just that, an imposter, an impersonator, a clone, a wannabe, a cause of heartbreak and real trouble. They are the ones who stand in front of the mirror and admire how good they look, how much they look like the real thing. Do they work hard? Never. Do they have unwavering faith in the team and their teammates? Never. Will they ever come through or deliver when you need them? Never. Do they care about performance? Never, as long as they can fool someone into believing they are the real thing. The reality is an impressionist in today's terminology would be termed "virtual."

We see these three types of people in our everyday world all the time. We need the players to change for the better. We need the impact players to make a difference so that the players will be encouraged. We do not need impressionists to drag us down or to be obstacles for others. We do not need them trying to deceive us into conforming to the behaviors of the world. The Bible says it this way for all players and impact players to hear,

> Do not conform to the pattern of this world, but be transformed by the renewing of your mind…
> — Romans 12:2

A mind changed by God will always change its course and not be fooled by the world's impersonators.

Understand if you are going to move forward and become a better player or an impact player, opponents (impressionists) will show up. They are usually people who want to keep power, position, or possessions (money). You are not getting this opposition because you are doing something wrong. You are getting it because you are doing something right (wanting to be a consistent player or readying yourself to be an impact player). Overcome the opposition by knowing you are on the right track, by remembering the Lord is for you, that you have a heart with the right motives. Check your motives. Do you want to impact your world for you or for Jesus? Jesus is the higher calling that impact players stay focused upon to accomplish any goal.

To become an impact player...

- Learn all you can learn about the area or subject you are trying to impact.

- Stay focused on the goal.

- Keep working.

- Don't listen to the impressionists (voices of opposition or imposters).

- Remember that any failure is an event, not a person.

- Every sinner has a past and every saint (Christ-follower) has a future. Maybe you need to start forgiving someone or yourself, so you can be all Christ would want you to be.

An impact player is like the righteous man that is mentioned in Proverbs 24:16,

> ...for though a righteous man falls seven times, he rises again...

Get up and get going! Let God show up and show through you. "Be strong and courageous." If you are a player, be better and stop doubting. If you are in impact player, let God be God!

- 18 -

If You Don't Like What
You Have Been Getting

Unhappy, dissatisfied, unfortunate, discontented, do any of these resonate within your being? If you don't like what you have been getting, let me ask you a question. What have you been giving? The Bible teaches us that a law is in place that says very clearly, "You reap what you sow."

> Do not be deceived; God cannot be mocked. A man reaps what he sows, The one who sows to please his sinful nature, from that nature will reap destruction; the one who sows to please the Spirit, from the Spirit will reap eternal life. Let us not become weary in doing good, for at the proper time we will reap a harvest if we do not give up.
> — Galatians 6:7-9

If you reap what you sow as the Bible states, the question is: what have you been sowing? Or if you do not like what you have been getting, look at what you have been giving! In the next few paragraphs let us look at some true stories of people I have known or pastored who didn't like what they were getting. Allow me to change the names to protect the guilty.

He stared at the diplomas on my office wall. The silence and the stare spoke volumes about the depth of trouble, grief, and pent up anger he was carrying around. Finally I said, "Pete, what is going on in your world?"

"How about a list of what is going wrong," was his response.

"Okay, let me hear about that list," I said.

"You do not have enough time to hear the list," he said.

"Go ahead, try me," I said while trying to hide my thoughts that "you are probably right" because I already knew some of the things on his list.

"My adult kids won't talk to me anymore. For the two oldest it has been almost two years. For the others it has been several months. My wife says she is done. My business is drying up. There isn't much income anymore. My mother says that since Dad died she hasn't seen me enough. My health insurance has dropped me because they say I have cost them too much with all my unnecessary trips to emergency room and doctors. My truck is about to be repoed. The house may go to foreclosure. All of my former friends treat me like I've got some contagious, fatal disease. Do I need to go any further?"

"No," I replied. You see I knew Pete. Pete was getting what he been sowing. His wife and one of his adult sons, as well as a business associate, had all been in to see me regarding Pete and his treatment of them.

Pete had made unreal demands of his sons and when they weren't able to come through even though they had tried, Pete's anger and his wrath, would explode upon them. One day they said to each other, "Enough. We are done talking to dad. We are not going to deal with him and his unreal expectations anymore." Pete had sown anger, wrath and unreal expectations that ended up in verbal arguments that almost came to physical blows. Pete's wife had received the same but it had gone further when her trust of Pete's fidelity was broken. She had decided the broken vows put the finishing touches on twenty plus years of marriage. Divorce papers were served. Pete's business associates were fed up with the scams and the lies. The closest one served Pete notice that he was done. "I'm cutting my losses, and you and I are through doing business together." Yes, Pete was reaping what he had sown. You see, not only do we reap what we sow; we reap the kind we have sown. For example, if I plant Jonathan apples in time I will reap Jonathan apples, not MacIntosh apples. In other words if your talk is angry, you'll get angry words back at you.

Let me tell you about a spoiled teenage girl that was musically very gifted. She had exceptional musical talent that resonated from her voice to the variety of instruments she could play. She knew she was good. She acted like she was too good to talk to or be around the other teen girls. Her mother added to the mystique by bragging on her and giving her whatever she asked. But one night she told her mother that she wanted to go out to party with a certain boy. For the first time the mother said "no." The girl's wrath exploded on her mom and then turned into months of horror. You see the daughter jumped out of a speeding car. She suffered tremendous injuries, especially to her head. No one expected her to live or walk again. She did live and after years began to walk with a limp and speak with a slur, sometimes a non-understandable sentence or phrase. She had sown the seeds of "I don't need anyone. I am better than everyone." She reaped the consequences: humbled and alone.

Today if you are not experiencing forgiveness, have you forgiven? If you are not experiencing healthy relationships, have you fostered friendships? If you have a communication problem with someone, have you been communicating? If you would say "no one loves me," have you been giving love? Yes, we decide what we will reap!

- 19 -

If You Are Not Dead, You Are Not Done

At eighteen this healthy boy just knew his life was over. He did not want to turn 18 and have to be responsible for his life choices. He stayed in his room thoroughly depressed. This type of walking dead happens at a variety of ages. For some it is 21 or 30 or 40 or 50 or 60 or 70 or _ ? The attitude that life has escaped you can sneak up on anyone at any age. This brings us to "if you are not dead, you are not done."

I have a high tech message for you. Whether you get the message by a tweet, a text, an email, a voicemail, a blog or a recent Facebook entry, please get the communication. Maybe it will come through a retro social medium like snail mail, or a landline talk, a fax or a face-to-face interaction. So whether someone uses a cellphone or a twitter account, the message is still the same. If you are breathing, you are not done. If you are reading this, you are not done. If you pinch yourself and feel it, you are not done.

Maybe you need to find God's purpose for you to keep on keeping on; you know, really living! It is what God wants because you are still here. He wants you! He needs you to fulfill His purpose for you. It is your choice to live, to finish what has been started in you. If you are living, you are giving. But if you are in the "death-mode" mindset, then you are consuming not giving. You are indifferent and uncaring. You are spiritually flat-lined. You haven't heard from God for a long, long time. You haven't focused or fixed your eyes on Jesus in months.

Maybe we should write your obituary with the title: *I Died Today and Nobody Noticed.*

> Today I died and nobody noticed. Since I didn't have time to text or tweet, it will take a while before anyone realizes my blog is obsolete. By that time any hard drive memory of my being will have been purged to make space available for more important use. Maybe it will be my lack of new friends on Facebook that will say something is wrong, that I am gone? Will there be any missed calls on my cell log? Will my lack of fax proclaim my swan song? Could it be that e-mail will prevail to pass along my demise? It is delusional to think anyone here in this 21st century place would be cognizant of my departure. Yes, this 20th century born man died today. You didn't ask why? But your stare seems to be asking where? My reply regarding my demise to where is very simplified... *at church.*

All too often that would be too true for why we see so many walking dead who have no purpose, who are doing nothing.

Dead churches assassinate many attenders. If the man in the pulpit isn't alive in Christ, death fills the pews. I've been surprised with previous colleagues, pastors, that confessed to no regular alone time with God (whether reading the Bible or in prayer). If you are not listening to God, interacting with God, it is logical that you probably lack direction (purpose) that brings life to your brain and bones. Some allow death to be their focus because of the past. Let me tell you about a lady who couldn't get past her past.

The call came to me when I was pastoring First church. The adult daughter was extremely shaken that her mother would die before she could see her again. She lived in a large city and the travel would take a few hours. "Pastor," she said, "my mother is dying and the doctors told me they didn't know how long she would be alive. They told me that she might not live until I could arrive. She has lived a hard, sinful life. I know you don't know mom or me, but would you go and try to lead her to Christ so I could see her again?"

"Of course, which hospital is she in and what is her name?" (Cold gospel calls can be very difficult because the person you are sharing with doesn't know you.)

Upon arriving at Agnes's room she was barely conscious. Lifeless doesn't even describe her. I prayed before I entered the room knowing from her daughter that she had lived a hard, sinful life and wanted nothing to do with God or church. I introduced myself. Agnes' eyes shot daggers at me. The profanity flowed as she told me to leave her room.

"I know you're here because my goody-two-shoes daughter must have called you."

I found myself standing steadfast next to the head of her hospital bed and saying, "That is correct. She wants to see you again and if you go to hell because you haven't asked forgiveness for your sins and asked Christ into your heart, she knows she won't see you." (Wow, Lord, did I just say that?)

"That can't happen. I have too many sins for Him to forgive me!"

"So, you are calling Jesus a liar? You are saying you do not believe the Bible to be truth?"

"If I wasn't so weak, I'd get out of this bed and beat the ** out of you, preacher!?

"You did say you were too sinful to be saved, didn't you?" Silence. "Well that is what I heard from you Agnes and that says Jesus is a liar." (I'm glad no nurses or doctors were nearby.)

"Why are you saying that, preacher?"

"Agnes, I am saying that because the Bible says,

> For God so loved the world (you and me) that He gave His one and only Son that whoever believes in Him shall not perish but have eternal life. For God did not send His Son into the world to condemn the world, but to save the world (you and me) through Him. Whoever believes in Him is not condemned.
> — John 3:16-18a

That is one reason I'm saying you are calling Jesus a liar. That scripture tells us you can be saved because whoever doesn't mean everybody can, except Agnes! More silence as she continued to look at me in disbelief. The Bible also tells us,

> If we confess our sins, He is faithful and just and will forgive our sins and purify us from all unrighteousness.
> — 1 John 1:9

Agnes, if you ask Jesus to forgive your sins, and come into your heart, you will make it to Heaven!"

"How can you be so sure?"

"Agnes, Jesus said it. He even told the one thief on the cross next to Him, 'Today, you will be with me in Paradise.' That thief couldn't go back and do anything about his past, sinful life. He could only ask Jesus to 'remember me.' So it is Jesus' response to him and to others that make me certain you can go to Heaven."

This hardened, sinful woman looked away and when she turned back toward me her eyes were full of tears. "What do I do?" said Agnes.

"Are you ready to ask God to forgive and ask Christ into your heart?"

"Yes!"

I led Agnes in the sinner's prayer. She received Christ. I read a few verses of assurance and she said, "I will see my daughter again."

And it is just like God to allow Agnes to live a few days so that she and her daughter could have some special moments on earth all the while knowing they would be together again.

He was known as the town drunk of Buffalo, Oklahoma. He had never walked with the Lord but now face to face with the doctor's comments. "You have terminal cancer. There is nothing we can do to heal you." Sobering words for a man who spent his adult years inebriated. His mind kept playing back "terminal cancer" and "there is nothing we can do." His life had kept his family from darkening church doors. I met them after receiving a call from his sister who lived in Chicago. She told me about Leonard and his alcoholic life, about his not being ready to face eternity, and about his large, extended family who didn't know Jesus. Her plea was for me to go and to try to share the salvation plan of Jesus to her brother. I reassured her that I would go with that purpose.

As I approached Leonard's hospital room the hallway was literally full of people. Inching my way through the crowd to reach the door, I thought "this man has a lot of people who care about him." As I worked my way into the room and got close to the head of Leonard's hospital bed, I introduced myself to Leonard.

"Your sister from Chicago called to see if I would come and pray for you."

Leonard's response was, "That is just like Georgia. She has loved me no matter what I did or how many drinks I had downed."

"That is great to have someone in your family that loves you like that."

"It really is," said Leonard. "Well, you go ahead and pray for me, preacher."

"Leonard, I will but before I do can I explain something to you? I know from your sister what the doctor has told you. I also know when we face death the question, "what if there is a Heaven and hell" comes to people's minds. What if there is an eternity to spend beyond the life on earth? These questions are answered in the Bible. There is an eternity. There is a destination of your choosing, Heaven or hell." I went on to explain how Jesus died, paid the price for sins so that anyone who asks forgiveness and receives Jesus in his/her heart will have eternal life or eternal damnation if he rejects Jesus here and then dies.

Leonard's eyes were watery. I also noticed that the room had mostly emptied of people.

"Leonard, do you want to choose Jesus and have eternal life?"

Without hesitation, without arguments Leonard's response was "Yes. I've wasted my life here." While witnessing a blessed, Holy Spirit-filled time of Leonard receiving Christ, I could hear others sobbing in the hallway. Some of the family had heard and were also moved by God.

"Thank you, Lord Jesus, for your love and for never giving up on trying to reach your creation," I said.

Leonard said "Thank you, Jesus." My heart was pounding with joy.

"Leonard, what else can I do for you," I asked.

Leonard said, "Pray for me that I will get well enough to go home for a short time before I die so that I can go to church and also tell my family and drinking buddies about Jesus."

"I can do that," I said.

I often wished I could have been in that church to watch the preacher's face, as well as the faces of the regular church attenders, the day Leonard walked through the front doors along with 28 family members and five of his old drinking buddies.

We need to make our decisions for Jesus and follow Him before we face our last moments on earth. Even though Leonard had received "terminal cancer" from the doctor's words, he hadn't died yet. In his last few short days on earth his life was radically changed from alcoholic to agent for Jesus. Several family members and friends came to Christ because of Leonard's conversion and the fact that as long as he was breathing he had a purpose.

Remember life on earth is very short in comparison to eternity. The Bible says we are like

> ...a mist that appears for a little while and then vanishes. Instead, you ought to say, if it is the Lord's will, we will live to do this or that.
> — James 4:14b-15

God also tells us if we have the strength "...the length of our days is seventy years or eighty." In that time span it tells us there will be trouble and sorrow but "...they will quickly pass and we will fly away" (Psalm 90:10).

Don't wait until the last few days of your life on earth to experience Jesus. You are not really living without Him, only existing. This mortal body and these brief seconds on planet earth are both temporary. Think on the eternal and make your choice. Don't waste any more mental, emotional, or spiritual energy on the temporary! God has a purpose for the rest of your life on earth, no matter how brief or how long that may be.

- 20 -

Facing Your *If* Victoriously

There are many more *if*, *if only*, and *what if* scenarios that could be written. You could probably add a few chapters of your own to *Facing the If in Life*. The question before us is: is it possible, truly possible to face your *if* and emerge victorious? The answer is with God, an emphatic "Yes!" Where does your victory over *if* begin? It starts in your mind. It travels that 14 to 16 inch highway to the heart. When your mind is renewed because it is in sync with your heart the road to winning over *if* has begun.

If you let your thinking become prisoner to the problem(s) you are facing, *if* will launch missiles that will randomly cause you to focus on the negatives. But if you choose to allow God to renew your mind by seeking Him in every situation *if* presents, you will become God-focused on the possibilities that are positive.

> Do not conform any longer to the pattern of this world, but be transformed by the renewing of your mind. Then you will be able to test and approve what God's will is— His good, pleasing and perfect will.
> — Romans 12:12

Too many times in over 35 years of ministry I have been told *if* I could only know God's will maybe I would have peace and be able to optimistically face my *ifs*! To be victorious over *if* means you will not only have optimism, but also peace…peace about you and God's will! You can know His general will (if you would allow me to say it this way) and His specific will for you each day, every hour that you live. You can have His peace which translates into being victorious over your *ifs*. His general will for all of us is written down in the Bible. You need to read and heed what the Bible says. Learn it. Read it. Read it again and again and again….it will not get old! When you do this every day His general will, i.e. to forgive, to love one another, etc., becomes a part of you. Then when you talk to God, to Jesus, and to the Holy Spirit, you can rest upon the fact you are not alone. How? "Fix your eyes not on what is seen but on what is unseen" (2 Corinthians 4:18).

> We fix our eyes on Jesus, the Author and Perfector of our faith, who for the joy set before Him endured the cross, scorning its shame, and sat down at the right hand of the throne of God. Consider Him who endured such opposition from sinful men (with a lot of 'ifs, if only & what ifs'), so that you will not grow weary and lose heart.
> — Hebrews 12:2-3

You and I can emerge as winners! You can know His specific will (what to do, how to respond, where to go, what path to follow), if you spend quality alone time with Him. Talk to the Holy Spirit. Listen. Ask for His leadership. Receive His instructions. Then with His peace, you choose to act, to do what you have to do. He will talk to you. You will need to make time so that you can listen. When He says, "Follow me," you will choose to follow. When He says, "Be strong and courageous"….for He is with you, you will, because you know as long as you hold His hand you will not fall. He not only has your back, He has you! You will not have to be anxious anymore, worry anymore, or be sleepless anymore if you are holding His hand. When we take His hand we are giving Him our weakness and we receive Him, His peace, and His strength. Trust and thankfulness replace our negative thoughts about *if, if only,* and *what if.* Why? Because our focus is on Him. To be victorious we hold His hand and like a child learning to walk, we take life a step at a time.

> The Lord gives strength to His people; the Lord blesses His people with peace.
>
> — Psalm 29:11

The choice that we make to be victorious is a recurring choice to "trust God" or not "to worry." We need to remember, He is

> ...an ever-present help in trouble. Therefore we will not fear, though the earth give way and the mountains fall into the heart of the sea.
>
> — Psalm 46:1-2

He tells us that He is "above all things," above all of our *ifs* in life. He is bigger than our pain. He is bigger than our concerns. To be victorious over our *ifs* starts with "Help. Help me, Jesus." He knows us. He wants to hear from us. He wants us to walk with Him, hand-in-hand through life's *ifs.* We need to choose Jesus. Trust Jesus. Lose ourselves from the inside out. Love God from the inside out.

What would that look like if you were retired, put out to pasture? It would mean enjoying the green grass! (After two years of drought here in Oklahoma I have almost forgotten what green grass looks like.) It would mean striving to get the "Benjamins" for security, would be replaced with securely trusting God! It would mean we would value relationships more than image for networking or connecting for impure motives. It means we have learned that "more" does not mean peace and happiness. It means we say, "God, search my heart, test my heart, and lead me" (Psalm 139). It means that we "do not merely listen to the word, and so deceive ourselves "but we "do what it says" (James 1:22). We can know the truth about facing our *ifs* in life and win. You see..."You will know the truth, and the truth will set you free." (John 8:3) Free from our ifs. Free from our negative thoughts. Free from our anxieties. Free! Free from self-deception. Free from the enemy's lies. Free from the past. Free from today. Free from tomorrow. Free! Victorious! A WINNER!

- 21 -

To Stay Victorious Over *If*

Now what do you do to stay free, to be at peace, to be a winner? What practical applications can you take hold of from the previous chapters?

Let us start with the first question "What do you do to stay at peace," free from anxieties, negative thoughts, etc. As stated, it starts with your choice to include God, Jesus, and the Holy Spirit in the everyday moment by moment life situations. It is taking God's hand and saying, "Okay, Lord, with You we can do this." Do what? Face your *if* head on by trusting God to hold you steady, to help you. You choose Him. You choose to trust Him. You listen to Him, His general and specific will for you each day. If you make those four choices, you will win with the Lord and yourself. You will have peace and freedom regardless of your pending problem(s). In other words, when you need God to get you out of a situation that you got into, when you need Him to turn your mistake into a miracle, He will be there for you. If your need is not intimidating to you, it may be insulting to God! You cannot intimidate God with your *if*. He doesn't make mistakes. He never says, "Oops!" The practical application is that the size of the need you face with life's *ifs* never overwhelms God. He doesn't go into distress mode or a Deity funk. He has a solution. It may not be pain free but it will be freeing. It will bring you peace. Once again it starts with you choosing to make Him your choice in life.

...the world offers a craving for physical pleasure, a craving for everything we see, and pride in our achievements and possessions. These are not from the Father, but are from this world. And this world is fading away, along with everything that people crave. But anyone who does what pleases God will live forever.

— 1 John 2:16-17

Therefore, to defeat the *if* in life we need to "focus on the unseen not the seen." We must not trade the ultimate for the immediate. (Read Esau and Jacob's story in Genesis 25:29-32) Have you traded away the ultimate for the now? What if you talked to God, asking forgiveness, letting Him know you desire Him and eternity with Him more than immediate gratifications? Do this and you win!

- 22 -

Biblical *IFs* and Choice

Facing the *if* in life isn't new, nor will it ever disappear. *If* is a huge Biblical word that appears to individuals and nations again and again because God gave choice to His creation, mankind. From God's first *if* in the garden with Adam and Eve to the present, *if* is all about our choices. "If you eat from this one tree....you will die" (one consequence). Allow me to give you several Biblical *ifs* in these next few pages. You will see they call for a choice and a trust that what God says, He does!

Solomon has finished the temple of the Lord and the Lord appeared to Solomon one night with this instruction for Israel, and all God's people.

> ....If my people, who are called by my name will humble themselves and pray and seek my face and turn from their wicked ways, then I will hear from heaven and will forgive their sin and will heal their land.
>
> — II Chronicles 7:14

Did you see the choices that people need to make? *If* they: 1. humble themselves, 2. pray, 3. seek His face, and 4. turn from their wicked ways. Four choices that will bring "forgiveness and healing." I like that but I also like what God says in verse 15.

> Now my eyes will be open and my ears attentive to the prayers....

He is watching and waiting to hear from those who will choose to do the four things needed. If you need healing, you know what to do. The U.S.A. needs to do this and receive His healing. We often hear "may God bless America." He has! We need to humble ourselves, seek His face, ask for mercy and listen to Him!

In the book of Proverbs chapter 2, the word *if* appears regarding gaining wisdom/understanding. This is key to facing life's *ifs*. Listen to the words of instruction as you read.

> My son, if you accept my words (there is choice again).....if you call out for insight and cry aloud for understanding (your choice)....if you look for it as for silver and search for it as for hidden treasure, (will you choose to take action?)....then you will understand the fear of the Lord and find the knowledge of God.
> — Proverbs 2:1-5

Later in the chapter He says,

> Then you will understand what is right and just and fair —every good path. For wisdom will enter your heart, and knowledge will be pleasant to your soul. Discretion will protect you, and understanding will guard you. Wisdom will save you....
> — Proverbs 2:9-12

Make the *if* choices and look at the promised benefits! Solomon had heard David instruct him with God's *if* word before. In I Chronicles 28:9 David says,

> And you, my son Solomon, acknowledge the God of your father, and serve him with wholehearted devotion and with a willing mind, for the Lord searches every heart and understands every motive behind the thoughts if you seek Him, He will be found by you; but if you forsake Him, He will reject you forever.

David was driving home the point to Solomon, it will be your choice how you respond to God's *if* and what the outcome will be.

One of my favorite *ifs* is found in the Old Testament book of Deuteronomy when the Lord is instructing Israel (as a nation) to be obedient about instructing their children—to following His decrees, etc. He tells them in Deuteronomy 4:24,

> ...if from there (wherever you worship Him) you seek the Lord your God, you will find Him if you look for Him with all your heart and with all your soul.

What a promise...choose to be unreserved in heart and soul when you seek God (no half-hearted, distracted effort) and you will find Him. I can testify it is a fundamental truth, a promise I hold onto in my life.

Now even though there are many more instructive *if* passages in the Old Testament like the clay and the potter in Jeremiah 18:5-10, let us look at some *ifs* in the New Testament.

Jesus and His disciples were walking from one town to another in order to preach the "good news" to the people. As they passed through a grain field the disciples picked a few heads of grain and began to eat because they were hungry. That sounds innocent enough, doesn't it? There was a problem. They were being watched (scrutinized) by a group of Pharisees who quickly confronted Jesus and the disciples with their "wrong" actions. "Your disciples are doing what is unlawful on the Sabbath." After giving them examples about David and his men entering the temple and eating on the Sabbath, Jesus says the following:

> I tell you that One greater than the temple is here. If you had known what these words mean, 'I desire mercy, not sacrifice,' you would not have condemned the innocent. For the Son of Man is Lord of the Sabbath.
>
> — Matthew 12:6-8

What an "if you had known!" How many times have we said, "If I had only known?" Jesus isn't finished as He drives home His point with verses 11-13.

> If any of you has a sheep and it falls into a pit on the Sabbath, will you not take hold of it and lift it out? How much more valuable is a man than a sheep! Therefore, it is lawful to do good on the Sabbath! Then He said to the man (who was in the synagogue and had a shriveled hand) "stretch out your hand." So he stretched it out and was completely restored, just as sound as the other.

The Pharisees—those legalists who are always watching for someone to step out of line—faced two big *ifs* from Jesus. "If you had only known" and "if any of you..." It has always amazed me during my last 35 plus years of ministry how many religious (watching) Pharisees there are in churches. It is astounding how rigid, how unloving, and how bloodthirsty they become!

Jesus rocks readers and listeners with some more big *ifs*. He certainly knows that people have to face *if* and make a choice in order to live.

> Then Jesus said to his disciples, "if anyone would come after me, he must deny himself and take up his cross and follow me. For whoever wants to save his life will lose it, but whoever loses his life for me will find it. What good will it be for a man, if he gains the whole world, yet forfeits his soul or what can a man give in exchange for his soul?"
>
> — Matthew 16:24-26

The choice Jesus presents with "if anyone" and "if he gains the whole world" is clear: if you follow me this is what it will cost you, and if you follow after the world the cost is your soul. Have you faced those *ifs*?

Maybe you are at the place of coming to Jesus with your *if*, like the leper in Mark 1:40. "A man with leprosy came to Jesus and begged him on his knees (see his desperation), 'If you are willing, you can make me clean.'" He doesn't lack trust in Jesus' ability to do for him what needs to be done. I wonder how many miracles and how many answers to prayer it took to get the leper to believe Jesus had the power. One of the great attributes of Jesus is His compassion.

> Filled with compassion, Jesus reached out his hand and touched the man. "I am willing," he said. "Be clean." Immediately the leprosy left him and he was cured.
> — Mark 1:41-42

It is vital to believe, to trust Jesus, and to know He will be compassionate with you and your *if*. Be like the woman with the severe bleeding problem in Mark 5:28 who thought "if I just touch His clothes, I will be healed." She chose to believe, when she acted upon her belief, she touched His clothes and she was healed!

If rattles around in our minds and hearts like an old freight train rumbling down the tracks to its station. If you think you are alive, you are only existing without Christ in your heart and in control. If you think your world is big, you haven't seen anything yet until you have Christ in it. You have a choice how you will face your *if(s)* in your life. You can either walk away from Christ and try to face *if* on your own or you can walk toward Christ, offer Him your hand, and face *if* with Jesus knowing He won't let go of you. If we will listen, God can be heard. If we choose childlike faith, that trust in Him will be key to a victorious life over the *ifs*.

If you are lost today, you can be found.

If you are tired of your old life, you can start a new one with Jesus.

If you need healing, you can be healed. Today is your day.

If you need a hand up, His hand is reaching out for you. Take hold of it!

If you have been caught unprepared (as my first book *Unprepared* stated) God is always prepared! See Jeremiah 7:5-7a.

Are you still wavering between going it alone or going with God to face your *ifs*? Maybe you need to hear what Elijah said to the people of Israel.

> "....How long will you waver between two opinions? If the Lord is God, follow Him; but if Baal (the world) is God, follow him.
> — I Kings 18:21

Facing the *if* in life is a choice! Joshua told Israel the same thing Elijah did. In Joshua chapter 24, he tells Israel to "fear the Lord and serve him with all faithfulness." He follows up that part of verse 14 with this in verse 15.

> But if serving the Lord is undesirable to you, then choose for yourselves this day whom you will serve,.... but as for me and my household, we will serve the Lord.

"I want to face my *if* in life with the Lord" is what Joshua was saying. Do you? I know I want the Lord holding my hand for any *if* that comes to me.

If God is weaning you from other dependencies where your trust has been misplaced, know this: If you choose to trust Him, you can rely upon His promise that:

> Neither height nor depth, nor anything else in all creation can separate you from God's loving Presence.
> — Romans 8:39

If you do not get a needed miracle, by the grace of God with faith in Him, be a miracle. (Read Nick Vujicic's book *Unstoppable.*)

Your *if* choice is faith or fear. Know God wants you to choose faith. That is why Jesus came. He made a way!

> If we confess our sins, He is faithful and just to forgive us our sins.
>
> — 1 John 4:9

He wants you to have His peace, His joy, and His love each step of your life. Remember when Jesus heals your hurts there may be some scars. But those scars say, "Healed." Move forward with life and its *ifs*. Do not let a scar hold you captive or keep you paralyzed. Jesus sets prisoners free. (See Psalm 146:7, John 8:32 and Romans 6:18.)

- 23 -

My Challenge For You

Do not limit God's ability to communicate to you by holding on to your *if*. God still speaks. He speaks through the Bible. He speaks through other wholly-devoted followers of Christ. He speaks through your alone prayer times...with thoughts that do not run amiss of His Word and His general will for you. We are needy. We need God. Our emotional DNA is made up of drive, needs, and awards. When you face the *if* in life, listen and look to God. He will help you even when the *if* seems overwhelming. He will be there! He will make a way!

When our miniature schnauzer, Annie, pursues the things of the world (outside our protective, fenced backyard) there is no stopping her. The smells and scents of her world all beckon her. Her behavior of "if I could just peruse that world...the world outside the fence or off the leash" is without fear while in hot pursuit of the squirrel or rabbit or _. The problem is her "I don't hear you" behavior (when you know she does hear you) will lead her to face a dangerous *if*. It happened like that not long ago when after running hard, single-focused on her worldly distraction for more than two miles. She found herself lost, afraid, and trembling. Does Annie sound like any of us when we face our *ifs* without God and His protection? You see, Annie knows when she is with my wife or me she is safe! Take my challenge. Walk with God and be safe when you face your *if(s)* in life.

The final chapter is yours to journal. Chapter 24 is for you to build your faith to face the *if(s)* in your life. Be sure to use it by summarizing your *if* and then telling how God got you through it.

- 24 -

Record Your *If(s)* and How
God Helped You Win!

Date	The *IF* you faced	Date	The Answer

Date	The *IF* you faced	Date	The Answer

About the Author

Dr. Robert J. Shephard is an ordained elder and wholly-devoted servant of Jesus Christ. Bob has been a minister for over 35 years. He is also the author of *Unprepared* which has been read world-wide. His spiritual journey began in public education at the secondary level where he served as head football and baseball coach, as well as athletic director and assistant superintendent of schools. Bob has been a senior pastor for five churches, as well as serving in district leadership on various boards and ministry assignments. He earned a B.S. degree from Olivet Nazarene University, and M.A. from Western Michigan University. He also holds an honorary D.D. from Berean College. Dr. Shephard is happily married to his high school sweetheart. They have four children and 13 grandchildren.